Niccolò di Giovanni Fiorentino
and Venetian Sculpture
of the Early Renaissance

The publication of this monograph
has been aided by a grant from the
Samuel H. Kress Foundation

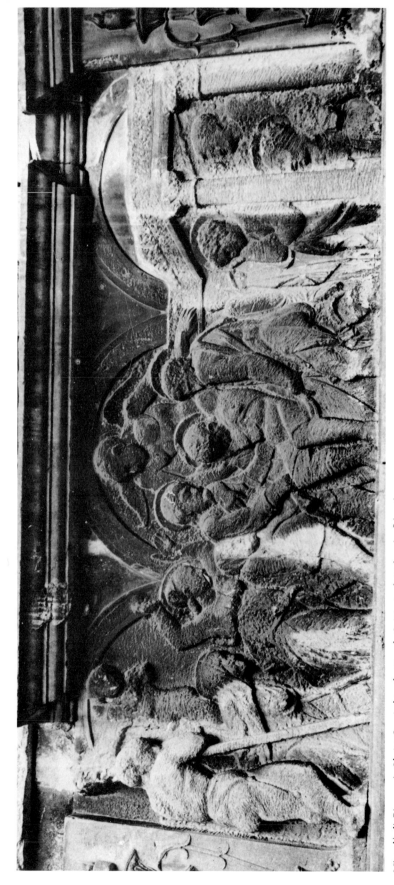

Niccolò di Giovanni, Christ Carried to the Tomb, S. Maria di Valverde, Šibenik

ANNE MARKHAM SCHULZ

Niccolò di Giovanni Fiorentino and Venetian Sculpture of the Early Renaissance

PUBLISHED BY

NEW YORK UNIVERSITY PRESS

for the College Art Association of America

NEW YORK 1978

Monographs on Archaeology and Fine Arts
sponsored by
THE ARCHAEOLOGICAL INSTITUTE OF AMERICA
and
THE COLLEGE ART ASSOCIATION OF AMERICA
XXXIII
Editor
Isabelle Hyman

Library of Congress Cataloging in Publication Data
Schulz, Anne Markham, 1938–
   Niccolo di Giovanni Fiorentino and Venetian sculpture of the
early Renaissance.

   (Monographs on archaeology and fine arts; 33)
   "Digest of documents concerning the life and works of Niccolò
di Giovanni Fiorentino": p.
   1. Niccolò di Giovanni Fiorentino.   2. Sculptures—Italy—
Biography.   3. Sculpture, Renaissance—Italy—Venice.
I. College Art Association of America.   II. Title.   III. Series.
NB623.N515S38   730'.92'4 [B]   77-6903
ISBN O-8147-7786-4

Manufactured in the United States of America

For Juergen

Contents

Preface

THE STUDY of Venetian sculpture has been neglected for too long. No doubt the recent appearance of Wolfgang Wolter's monumental corpus of Venetian Gothic sculpture will make a difference. But it is in the nature of such a work to pose questions—not to answer them—and it is precisely answers which the study of Venetian Quattrocento sculpture so desperately wants. No monograph exists on any of the major figures of the century—indeed, it is too soon to write one. General surveys of the history of Italian sculpture customarily betray both ignorance and lack of interest in Venetian Quattrocento sculpture. Publications in the field are mainly limited to locally issued journals, some of which are nearly inaccessible outside Venice. To this day Venetian sculpture has remained almost entirely a province of local scholars: it is to them we owe almost everything we know. The earliest students of the subject were Leopoldo Cicognara, Giannantonio Moschini, and Pietro Selvatico, writing in the first half of the nineteenth century. Concerned primarily with questions of style, they relied for basic information chiefly on tradition as preserved in early guides and biographies of artists. The cultivation of archival studies by Venetians of the second half of the nineteenth century put the subject on a new footing. In 1868 Giambattista Lorenzi brought forth a corpus of documents concerning the construction and decoration of the Ducal Palace. In 1893 Pietro Paoletti published over a thousand documents in his *L'architettura e scultura del rinascimento in Venezia*. Provided with a collection of specially made photographs and drawings and accompanied by a text which treated the sculpture of an entire century, from ca. 1400 to the early sixteenth century, with exhaustive completeness and a sure sense of quality and style, his book seems the work, not of a single man, but of an entire generation. It is not hard to imagine how daunted Paoletti's colleagues must have felt by his achievement. Indeed, apart from a couple of stunning archival discoveries by Gino Fogolari and Rodolfo Gallo and the rediscovery by Leo Planiscig and Giovanni Mariacher of a few lost works, subsequent contributions to the study of Venetian Quattrocento sculpture have been few and insignificant when they have not actually introduced errors or obfuscated issues which formerly were clear. It is no exaggeration to say that the study of Venetian Quattrocento sculpture is now where the study of Florentine art was half a century ago.

Yet Venetian sculpture deserves better. Granted, not all of it is of the highest quality. Most Venetian fifteenth-century sculpture is less highly finished than contemporary Florentine sculpture, for, intended for the out-of-doors, it used a less crystalline, if more resistant, stone. In spite of that its condition is often deplorable. But the best pieces of Venetian statuary and relief are as expressive and as technically expert as the best pieces executed anywhere. And even if Venetian sculpture could not make this claim, still it would be of the utmost historical importance to determine what sort of art was being commissioned by the richest, the most populous and powerful republic in the Renaissance.

But if Venetian sculpture has been neglected, how shall we characterize the study of Dalmatian Quattrocento sculpture? Short of going to Dalmatia, of searching out custodians with keys to long-forsaken churches, of begging for permission to see reliefs moved for safe-keeping to monastery bedrooms or directors' offices, there is no way a student can begin to learn about Dalmatian sculpture. Since the important work of Dagobert Frey and Hans Folnesics at the beginning of the century hardly an article has appeared on the subject not written in Serbo-Croatian and not published in books and journals found only in the libraries of Yugoslavia. Photography of Dalmatian monuments by the Yugoslavs themselves has only recently begun: time and again one must turn to the Austrian publications of the turn of the century for the only, generally inadequate, reproduction of a key monument.

Yet the study of Dalmatian sculpture well repays the effort. In the fifteenth century Dalmatian sculpture experienced a real flowering. In large part Dalmatia benefited from the prosperity of Venice, whose colony most of it became in 1420. Venice had no stone of its own; stone used in Venice for architectural details and sculpture came primarily from Istria and the Dalmatian islands. Where quarries abound there will exist dynasties of masons. Venice had no indigenous tradition of stone-carving; in Dalmatia entire male populations devoted themselves to the practice of this art. The shops of the Venetian *tagliapiere* welcomed the Dalmatians who flocked in number to the capital. To Venice came Giorgio da Sebenico and Giovanni Dalmata. Francesco Laurana worked at Urbino. Dalmatian sculptors are documented as far afield as Hungary. But most of them remained at home: the number of lesser artisans whose names and biographies are known to us is legion. At Šibenik and Trogir, on Pag and Rab, they were employed to execute the myriad projects of construction and embellishment conceived on so ambitious a scale that the communities which launched them rarely could afford to finish them. For these projects noted architects and sculptors, of whom Michelozzo is only the best known, were sometimes summoned from afar. Its own historical importance, therefore, more than justifies the study of Dalmatian sculpture. But the student of Italian sculpture reaps unexpected rewards. Archival material, whose wholesale destruction in Venice presents a real obstacle to the understanding of Venetian Quattrocento art, is preserved in Yugoslavia in extraordinary abundance. This makes it possible to gain in Dalmatia insights into the careers of artists, all written trace of whom has disappeared at Venice. So it was for me with Niccolò di Giovanni Fiorentino.

In the writing of this book a major concern was the presentation of a complete corpus of photographs of the Venetian monuments whose attribution I attempt. Not one of the works had ever been reproduced properly. The unscalable height at which most of the works I was dealing with are found did not present the least of my problems. Fortunately, the Soprintendenza ai Monumenti had just concluded a campaign of restoration, complete with photographic records, of the statue of *St. Christopher* at the Madonna dell'Orto, while old negatives of the statues of the Arco Foscari existed in the photographic archives of the Ducal Palace. But at the Foscari Tomb in the Frari and the Capello Tomb at S. Elena scaffolds had to be built. The opportunity to examine the monuments minutely from close quarters provided a number of striking insights whose significance, I hope, will emerge from this book. The scaffolds also permitted the recording of images possibly not seen since the components of the tombs left the sculptor's workshop. Comparative photographs of Dalmatian monuments were mostly made anew at my request by the Superintendency of Monuments at Split. For this courtesy I express my deepest thanks.

I also wished to see whether any archival material on the monuments in question was to be newly discovered in the Venetian archives. I was fortunate in finding new documents relating to the Giustiniani Tomb, but repeated searches yielded not so much as the name of Niccolò di Giovanni. This is not to be wondered at, given the loss of all records (apart from statutes) of the stonecarvers' guild as well as the supervising governmental body of the *Giustizia vecchia* for the period of the Renaissance. But all published documents concerning Niccolò Fiorentino were assiduously tracked down and translated.

Accumulating the relevant bibliography in Serbo-Croatian proved the most arduous and frustrating of my labors. I am grateful to my Yugoslav colleagues, Dr. Kruno Prijatelj, director of the Galerija Umjetnina at Split, and Dr. Cvito Fisković, director of the Superintendency of Monuments at Split, for sending me unique exemplars of their publications, and to the latter for permitting me to borrow repeatedly from the library of the Superintendency at Split. The director of the Naučna Biblioteka at Split, Prof. Hrvoje Morović, was invariably helpful. But most of all this project owes its success to the devotion of my translators, Mr. Pierre Djokić at Princeton and Mr. Igor Silić and Miss Liana Župevć at Venice, whose readiness to help on all occasions can never be adequately repaid.

Without the assistance of so many others this project might never have been brought to completion. At Venice I am indebted to Soprintendente alle Gallerie dott. Francesco Valcanover, Soprintendente ai Monumenti arch. Renato Padoan, former director of the Museo Civico Correr Prof. Terisio Pignatti, former director of the Centro tedesco di studi veneziani Dr. Wolfgang Wolters, Padre Luciano Marini, Prior of S. Maria dei Frari, and Dott.ssa Lina Frizziero. I shall never forget the day spent with Mr. Davor Domančić of the Superintendency at Split tramping the goat paths of Brač in search of long-abandoned churches with sculptures from the school of Niccolò Fiorentino or scaling Mount Marjan with his colleague, Mrs. Ksenija Cicarelli, to find the hermitage with Aleši's relief of St. Jerome. For the expenditure of much time and effort I am immensely grateful to Prof. Ivo Petricioli of the University of Zadar; to Mrs. Edda Portolan of the Dubrovački Muzej; to Mr. Ivo Babić, director of the Muzej grada at Trogir. Prof. Robert Munman and Dr. Wolfgang Wolters kindly provided me with photographs. Prof. George Stričević generously found and translated articles for me. Not least, I owe a debt of gratitude to my husband, without whose stimulus and encouragement I, too, should be numbered among those answerable for the neglect of Venetian sculpture. It is therefore fitting that this book be dedicated to him.

This work has received the financial support of the Howard Foundation (1972–73) and the Samuel H. Kress Foundation, the American Council of Learned Societies, and the American Philosophical Society (1974–75), for which I am very grateful.

Providence, R.I.

List of Illustrations

The attributions of Figs. 1 through 76 are the author's own and are made here for the first time.

Abbreviations

Raised Arabic numerals preceding the date of publication indicate edition.

ASV   Archivio di Stato, Venice

Bibl. Marc.   Biblioteca Marciana, Venice

Mus. Cor.   Museo Civico Correr, Venice

Arslan, *Ven. got.*, 1970   Edoardo Arslan, *Venezia gotica*, Venice, 1970

Burckhardt, *Cic.*, ¹1855   Jacob Burckhardt, *Der Cicerone*, Basel, ¹1855

Burckhardt-Bode, *Cic.*, ⁵1884   Burckhardt, *Der Cicerone*, with W. Bode, Leipzig, ⁵1884

Burckhardt-Bode-Fabriczy, *Cic.*, ⁷1898   Burckhardt, *Der Cicerone*, with W. Bode and C. von Fabriczy, Leipzig, ⁷1898

Cicogna, *Delle inscrizioni*   Emmanuele Antonio Cicogna, *Delle inscrizioni veneziane*, Venice, i, 1824; ii, 1827; iii, 1830; iv, 1834; v, 1842; vi, 1853

Cicognara, ii, 1816   Leopoldo Cicognara, *Storia della scultura dal suo risorgimento in Italia sino al secolo xix*, Venice, ii, 1816

Egg *et al.*, *Oberitalien Ost*, ¹1965   Erich Egg, Erich Hubala, Peter Tigler, Wladimir Timofiewitsch, Manfred Wundram, *Oberitalien Ost* (Reclams Kunstführer, ed. M. Wundram, *Italien*, ii), Stuttgart, ¹1965

Fiocco, *Dedalo*, 1927-28   Giuseppe Fiocco, "I Lamberti a Venezia—I, Niccolò di Pietro," *Dedalo*, viii, 1927-28, pp. 287-314; "II, Pietro di Niccolò Lamberti," *ibid.*, pp. 343-376; "III, Imitatori e seguaci," *ibid.*, pp. 432-458

Fogolari, *Pal. Duc.*   Gino Fogolari, *Il Palazzo Ducale di Venezia*, Milan, n.d.

Fogolari, *L'arte*, 1930   Fogolari, "Gli scultori toscani a Venezia nel quattrocento e Bartolomeo Bon Veneziano," *L'arte*, xxxiii, 1930, pp. 427-465

Folnesics, *Jahrb. Zentralkomm.*, 1914   Hans Folnesics, "Studien zur Entwicklungsgeschichte der Architektur und Plastik des XV. Jahrhunderts in Dalmatien," *Jahrbuch des kunsthistorischen Institutes der k. k. Zentral-kommission für Denkmalpflege*, viii, 1914, pp. 27-196

Frey-Molè   Dagobert Frey, "Der Dom von Sebenico und sein Baumeister Giorgio Orsini," with an appendix of documents by Vojeslav Molè, *Jahrbuch des kunsthistorischen Institutes der k. k. Zentral-kommission für Denkmalpflege*, vii, 1913, pp. 1-169

Fulin-Molmenti, *Guida*, 1881   R. Fulin and P. G. Molmenti, *Guida artistica e storica di Venezia e delle isole circonvicine*, Venice, 1881

Gallo, *Atti Ist. ven.*, 1961-62   Rodolfo Gallo, "L'architettura di transizione dal gotico al rinascimento e Bartolomeo Bon," Venice. Istituto veneto di scienze, lettere ed arti. *Atti* (Classe di scienze morali e lettere), cxx, 1961-62, pp. 187-204

Grevembroch, *Mon. Ven.*   Johannes Grevembroch, *Monumenta Veneta ex antiquis ruderibus*, i, 1754; ii, 1754; iii, 1759 in Venice, Museo Civico Correr, Raccolta Gradenigo-Dolfin, MS. 228

Lorenzetti, ¹1926   Giulio Lorenzetti, *Venezia e il suo estuario*, Venice et al., ¹1926

Mariacher, *Le arti*, 1940-41   Giovanni Mariacher, "Note su Antonio da Righeggio e Antonio Rizzo," *Le arti*, iii, 1940-41, pp. 193-198

Mariacher, *Arte veneta*, 1948   Mariacher, "Profilo di Antonio Rizzo," *Arte veneta*, ii, 1948, pp. 67-84

Mariacher, *Pal. Duc.*, 1950   Mariacher, *Il Palazzo Ducale di Venezia*, Florence, 1950

Mariacher, *BM*, 1950   Mariacher, "New Light on Antonio Bregno," *Burlington Magazine*, xcii, 1950, pp. 123-128

Mariacher, *Diz. bio.*, xii, 1970   Mariacher, "Bono, Bartolomeo," *Dizionario biografico degli italiani*, Rome, xii, 1970, pp. 275-277

Meyer, *JPK*, 1889   Alfred Gotthold Meyer, "Das venezianische Grabdenkmal der Frührenaissance," *Jahrbuch der preussischen Kunstsammlungen*, x, 1889, pp. 79-102 and 187-208

Moschini, 1815   Giannantonio Moschini, *Guida per la città di Venezia*, Venice, 1815

Mothes, *Geschichte*   Oscar Mothes, *Geschichte der Baukunst und Bildhauerei Venedigs*, Leipzig, i, 1859; ii, 1860

Munman, 1968

Robert Munman, *Venetian Renaissance Tomb Monuments*, Ph.D. dissertation, Harvard University, Cambridge, Mass., 1968 (typescript)

Munman, *BM*, 1971

Munman, "The Monument to Vittore Cappello of Antonio Rizzo," *Burlington Magazine*, cxiii, 1971, pp. 138-145

Paoletti, *Il fiore*

Ermolao Paoletti, *Il fiore di Venezia*, Venice, i, 1837; ii, 1839; iii, 1840; iv, 1840

Paoletti, 1893

Pietro Paoletti, *L'architettura e la scultura del rinascimento in Venezia*, Venice, 1893

Paoletti, "Bono," T-B, iv, 1910

P. Paoletti, "Bono, Bartolomeo di Giovanni," *Allgemeines Lexikon der bildenden Künstler*, ed. U. Thieme and F. Becker, Leipzig, iv, 1910, pp. 315-316; "Bono, Giovanni di Bertuccio," *ibid.*, pp. 317-318

Paoletti, "Bregno," T-B, iv, 1910

P. Paoletti, "Bregno, Antonio," *Allgemeines Lexikon der bildenden Künstler*, ed. U. Thieme and F. Becker, Leipzig, iv, 1910, pp. 568-569

Pincus, 1974

Debra Pincus, *The Arco Foscari: The Building of a Triumphal Gateway in Fifteenth Century Venice*, Ph.D. dissertation, New York University, New York, 1974 (typescript), reproduced in the Garland Series of Outstanding Dissertations in the Fine Arts, New York/London, 1976

Planiscig, *VB*, 1921

Leo Planiscig, *Venezianische Bildhauer der Renaissance*, Vienna, 1921

Planiscig, *VJ*, 1926

Planiscig, "Das Grabdenkmal des Orsato Giustiniani. Ein Beitrag zur Geschichte der venezianischen Skulptur im Quattrocento," *Jahrbuch der kunsthistorischen Sammlungen in Wien*, n.F. i, 1926, pp. 93-102

Planiscig, *VJ*, 1930

Planiscig, "Die Bildhauer Venedigs in der ersten Hälfte des Quattrocento," *Jahrbuch der kunsthistorischen Sammlungen in Wien*, n.F. iv, 1930, pp. 47-120

Planiscig, T-B, xxviii, 1934

Planiscig, "Rizzo, Antonio," *Allgemeines Lexikon der bildenden Künstler*, ed. U. Thieme and F. Becker, Leipzig, xxviii, 1934, pp. 408-410

Pohlandt, *BJ*, 1971

Wiebke Pohlandt, "Antonio Rizzo," *Jahrbuch der Berliner Museen*, xiii, 1971, pp. 162-207

Pope-Hennessy, *Ital. Goth. Sc.*, [1]1955

John Pope-Hennessy, *Italian Gothic Sculpture*, London, [1]1955

Pope-Hennessy, *Ital. Ren. Sc.*, [1]1958

Pope-Hennessy, *Italian Renaissance Sculpture*, London, [1]1958

Pope-Hennessy, *V & A Cat.*, 1964, i

Pope-Hennessy, *Catalogue of Italian Sculpture in the Victoria and Albert Museum*, London, 1964, i

Romanini, *Arte lombarda*, January–June 1964   Angiola Maria Romanini, "L'incontro tra Cristoforo Mantegazza e il Rizzo nel settimo decennio del Quattrocento," *Arte lombarda*, ix, pt. 1, January–June 1964 (*Studi in onore di Giusta Nicco Fasola*, i), pp. 91–102

Sansovino, 1581   Francesco Sansovino, *Venetia citta nobilissima et singolare, descritta in XIIII. libri*, Venice, 1581

Selvatico, *Sulla architettura*, 1847   Pietro Selvatico, *Sulla architettura e sulla scultura in Venezia dal medio evo sino ai nostri giorni*, Venice, 1847

Selvatico-Lazari, *Guida*, 1852   Selvatico and V. Lazari, *Guida artistica e storica di Venezia e delle isole circonvicine*, Venice/Milan/Verona, 1852

Seymour, *Sculpt.*, 1966   Charles Seymour Jr, *Sculpture in Italy: 1400 to 1500*, Harmondsworth, 1966

Venturi, *Storia*   Adolfo Venturi, *Storia dell'arte italiana*, Milan, vi, 1908; viii, pt. 2, 1924

Wolters, 1976   Wolfgang Wolters, *La scultura veneziana gotica (1300–1460)*, Venice, 1976

Zanotto, *Nuovissima guida*, 1856   Francesco Zanotto, *Nuovissima guida di Venezia e delle isole della sua laguna*, Venice, 1856

Zorzi, *Ven. scomparsa*, 1972   Alvise Zorzi, *Venezia scomparsa*, Milan, 1972

Introduction

BY 1450 VENICE had attained a position unrivaled by any state in Italy. Campaigns of the first half of the century, against the Carrara of Padua between 1404 and 1405 and the Visconti of Milan in the second quarter of the Quattrocento had resulted in Venetian acquisition of Vicenza, Verona, Padua, Dalmatia, Friuli and the Patriarchate of Aquileia, Bergamo and Brescia, Ravenna and Cremona. The Peace of Lodi of 1454 fixed Venetian boundaries at the Po to the south, at the Adda to the west. On the north Venetian territory extended beyond the foothills of the Alps; on the east it included Istria and the Dalmatian littoral. Even the concurrent advance of the Turks in the eastern Mediterranean did not substantially affect Venetian interests, for Venice, with its superior fleet, still retained possession of those cities whose strategic importance guaranteed the continuance of commerce. The Turks allowed Venetians free transit and commerce in their empire and Venetian galleys were no longer harassed by the Genoese, weaker now than they had ever been before. But in 1453 Constantinople fell to the Turks. In spite of the treaty signed the following year with Mohammed II, the course of Venetian history during the next quarter century was largely determined by the necessity of an adequate response to Ottoman aggression in the east.

The treaty of 1454 did not prevent Mohammed from annexing Thrace, Macedonia, and the kingdom of Trebizond or from ravaging Dalmatia and Albania. But it did delay a Venetian declaration of war until the fall of Argos in 1463, by which time, however, preparations for war had long been under way. Doge Francesco Foscari replied favorably to the advocacy by Pope Calixtus III (1455–58) of a crusade against the Turks, and Doge Cristoforo Moro (1462–71) was so far persuaded by the urgings of Pius II (1458–64) as to agree to accompany the crusade. During the principate of Pasquale Malipiero (1457–62) the Venetian *Signoria* decided to set aside each month 6,000 ducats from the proceeds of the salt tax for the needs of war. Modon, Coron, Nauplia, Negroponte, and Candia were fortified. In 1462 Metelino fell to the Turks. Galleys were armed—paid for with money drawn from the state funded debt. But this funding threatened to prove inadequate to the new financial burdens imposed by war, and in June 1463, after just two months of war, a measure was approved for a new *estimo* on the basis of which a tax, called the *decima*, was to be levied on the populace of Venice and the Veneto, thus giving, for the first time, a permanent and regular character to those direct taxes which hitherto had been levied only during extraordinary crises. Indeed, from 1464 until 1482 not a year passed in which there were not at least two *decime*. In August 1463 the preaching of Fra Michiel da Milano in the Piazza S. Marco netted 700,000 ducats for the cause of the crusade. In the spring of 1464 an attempt at the reconquest of Metelino led by Orsato Giustiniani failed. In August 1464 the pope, cardinals, and the doge assembled at Ancona in preparation for their departure for the Levant, but Pius's sudden death relieved the doge from the obligation of making the dreaded journey. Allied with Matthias Corvinus, whose kingdom was constant prey to the Turks, Venice continued to fight without assistance from sister states in Italy. In 1466 a Venetian armada under Vittore Capello took Athens but suffered a terrible defeat at Patras. A subsequent offer of peace was rejected by Mohammed. In 1467 the Turks were repulsed at Croia and Durazzo, but in the following year they conquered Armenia. The war continued until 1479, with major losses to Venice of Negroponte in 1470 and Scutari in 1478. But with the signing of a treaty in January 1479, Venetian commerce in the Ottoman Empire was immediately resumed, and within a short time Venice was once again enjoying a state of prosperity unequaled throughout Italy.

Despite the funneling of energy and money into the war in the Levant, intellectual and artistic activity did not cease at home. In 1460 a second chair in the humanities was founded at the School of St. Mark's. The first book printed in Venice bears the date of 1469, and in the course of the next decade Venice established herself as the capital of publishing in Europe. It is a measure of Venice's wealth that commissions for works of art did not abate. Large series of paintings were commissioned in the 1460s by the Scuola di S. Giovanni Evangelista, the Scuola di S. Marco, and the Scuola di S. Girolamo. Four triptychs were ordered for the newly completed church of S. Maria della Carità.

Nor is there any sign of a diminution in the volume of construction. Work went forward at S. Gregorio, S. Giobbe, S. Francesco del Deserto. S. Cristoforo della Pace was founded to commemorate the Peace of Lodi of 1454. S. Giorgio in Alga was finished in 1458; S. Giovanni in Olio was consecrated in 1463. A building campaign at S. Zaccaria, which envisaged both a restoration of the old church and the erection of a vast new basilica, was undertaken in 1458.

Mauro Codussi began construction of S. Michele in Isola in 1469. By 1457 the value of taxable real property in Venice appeared to have grown so much since 1425 that a new census was decreed. The *catasto*, not actually made till 1469, shows an increase in the value of taxable real property of approximately 20 percent, an excess of 6 percent over the rate of devaluation of the lira.[1] Although in 1461 the price of building material and labor was claimed to have fallen in respect to prices of a decade earlier,[2] wages of workmen in the building trades were so much higher in Venice than in Milan that Duke Francesco Sforza, who purchased an unfinished Venetian palace—the Ca' del Duca—in January 1461, was advised to hire workmen in Milan and to negotiate their monthly salaries before they left for Venice. Thus the duke was assured of saving perhaps a third of his labor costs. Salaries in Venice for such workers—"molto ingrosso, forsi el dopio, o al mancho el terzo più che non hano de la [in Milan]"[3]—explain the wave of immigration of foreign craftsmen which caused native stonemasons to complain of the scandals and inconveniences "per esser el dito mestier nele man de homeni che non sono de le terre de Venetiani." A statute incorporated into the constitution, or *Mariegola*, of the Venetian guild of stonecarvers on October 28, 1461, sought to redress the situation: by restricting the privileges of *maestri di bottega* to only those foreign master stonemasons who settled in Venice with their families, it limited the scope of activity of many foreign craftsmen.[4] Yet this did little to alleviate the pressures of foreign competition. Four years later members of the guild of *tagliapiere* lamented more piteously still that the importation of foreign works had reduced a formerly prosperous craft to "desolatin et destruction." On September 27, 1465, therefore, the guild prohibited the importation of works carved outside Venice under penalty of confiscation of the offending goods and a fine of 300 lire.[5] We know that Lombard stonecarvers were employed extensively on the reconstruction of the Ducal Palace after the fire of 1483. On October 12, 1486, the ducal councillors relaxed the statute of 1461 prohibiting foreign stonemasons who were not citizens *de intus* from trading in any product or appurtenance of their craft or keeping apprentices, after the *protomaestro* of the Ducal Palace, Antonio Rizzo, had testified that it was necessary for the construction of the palace that the Lombards remain.[6]

While this influx of foreign goods and workers reflects the greater expertise of stonemasons trained in Lombardy as well as cheaper prices for dressed stone abroad, it also indicates at home a healthy demand for stonework of all kinds—a demand apparently unaffected by the occasional inability of patrons to pay for what they had commissioned.[7] Indeed, commissions for sculpture in the late 1450s and 1460s in Venice not only do not give evidence of an economic decline but actually seem to have increased over the previous two decades. Under Doge Moro construction of the Arco Foscari—the monumental gateway leading from the courtyard of the Ducal Palace—was substantially completed and several life-size statues were set upon its pinnacles. At S. Marco the Doge provided for the erection of three altars, and the presbytery of S. Giobbe was built and ornamented with funds bequeathed by him. The choir screen of S. Maria dei Frari, finished in 1475, must at least have been designed by 1468 when Marco Cozzi inscribed the choir stalls. Tombs continued to be built. The scholar Paolo della Pergola (d. 1454) was honored by a sepulcher at S. Giovanni Elemosinario; the bishop of Vicenza, Pietro Miani (d. 1432), with a tomb at S. Maria dei Frari erected in 1464; Bartolomeo Morosini (d. 1444), with a tomb installed in S. Gregorio in 1468; Doge Foscari, with a monument at the Frari. It is not surprising, however, that the largest number of tombs erected during this period commemorated heroes of the war in the Morea, like Orsato Giustiniani and Vittore Capello.[8] Indeed, the Tomb of Pietro Mocenigo (d. 1476) in SS. Giovanni e Paolo reduced to insignificance Mocenigo's role as doge in its glorification of his exploits in the Turkish war.

The decade of the 1460s saw the close of the career of Bartolomeo Bon, recorded in 1460 as the foremost sculptor of the city.[9] From 1459 to 1460 Bon was employed on the construction of the lower part of the portal of SS. Giovanni e Paolo. In 1460 he was commissioned to execute the main portal with its statuary at the Madonna dell'Orto. Payments to Bon ceased at the end of a year's time but the portal was not finished until much later. Bon was also responsible for the design of the so-called Ca' del Duca, the palace begun in 1457 for Andrea Cornaro and sold soon afterward to Duke Francesco Sforza. Work on what would have been the largest private palace constructed at the time in Venice, however, was suspended because of the duke's impecuniosity when the palace had hardly risen above its foundations. There is record of Bon's employment in 1463 in the Ducal Palace. Very likely he was *protomaestro* in charge of the construction of the Arco Foscari for which he furnished the statue of *Arithmetic*. Bon died probably not long after making his will on August 8, 1464. From August 9, 1465, dates the death of his sometime partner, Pantaleone di Paolo. Evidently a reputed sculptor, Pantaleone is known to us only from a fragment of his much earlier Tomb of Jacopo della Torre from the Eremitani, Padua.[10] During this period Antonio Rizzo, lauded in epigrams by Gregorio Cornaro before 1464,[11] made his debut. One of the three carved altars in S. Marco for which he was paid by Doge Moro in 1469[12] is inscribed with the date of 1465. The commission for the Altars of St. Paul, St. James, and St. Clement was a prestigious one and is not likely to have been given to an artist who had not yet made his ability manifest. Pietro Lombardo is first documented in Padua in 1465, although he was probably already settled there at the beginning of 1464 when a contract for the acquisition of stone for the Tomb of Antonio Roselli in the Santo was signed. The tomb was installed in the spring of 1467,[13] but Pietro was still in Padua in September 1468.[14] It is not known precisely when he came to Venice; his arrival surely predates the earliest record of his presence there in 1474.[15]

During this period there was active in Venice another sculptor whose oeuvre proves him to have been a leading artist in his day. Among his commissions were three tombs—the Tombs of Doge Francesco Foscari, and the *Capitani Generali*, Orsato Giustiniani and Vittore Capello—which, by virtue of their size and lavishness and the prominence of the persons commemorated, count as major monuments. The five statues which this sculptor carved for the Arco Foscari of the Ducal Palace testify to the regard with which he was held by the Venetian *Signoria*. For the portal of the Madonna dell'Orto he executed the statue of *St. Christopher* at the behest of the Scuola di S. Maria e di S. Cristoforo. His relief of *St. Jerome* in S. Maria del Giglio was probably purchased by a Venetian nobleman. The dating of these works does not constitute a vital problem: all fit comfortably within the decade 1457–68. But their authorship is among the most vexed questions confronting the student of Quattrocento sculpture. While stylistic links between some of the monuments have occasionally been noted, they have never been perceived as all belonging to a single stylistic group. Nor has any one of them ever been attributed correctly. Indeed, the most famous of them—the Tomb of Doge Francesco Foscari—parades as a work of an artist whose very existence has never been confirmed by any document. Such confusion is easily explained. Documents provide no clue whatever to the authorship of these works, and early secondary sources name sculptors who cannot otherwise be traced. Therefore, the evidence available for attribution is mainly visual—alas, notoriously unreliable. To be sure, in the case of our master iconographical evidence also plays an important part, while historical information serves to buttress conclusions arrived at independently. But it is ultimately on the basis of data of a necessarily subjective nature that I shall attempt to prove, first, that the works under consideration were designed, if not invariably executed, by a single sculptor; and second, that that sculptor was Niccolò di Giovanni Fiorentino who, as *capomaestro* of the Cathedral at Šibenik, sculptor and architect of the Orsini Chapel at Trogir, author of numerous works of statuary and relief dispersed among the churches and museums of the Yugoslav coast, was the major sculptor and architect in Dalmatia from his arrival there in 1467 until his death in 1505.

The period of Niccolò's activity in Venice coincides with the transition from a Gothic to a Renaissance style of architecture. The transition did not proceed according to an orderly progression: rather, Gothic and Renaissance forms cohabit, often within a single monument. The base of the colossal order which articulates the diamond rustication of the *pianterreno* of the Ca' del Duca possesses a Gothic spur. The massive columns pillaged from Torcello which flank the portal of SS. Giovanni e Paolo are accompanied by slender twisted colonnettes. The monumental triumphal arch erected at the entrance to the Arsenal in 1460 was succeeded in time by the Gothic churches of S. Andrea della Zirada and S. Giovanni in Bragora; the classical design of the Ca' del Duca was succeeded by the Gothic Palazzo

Soranzo–van Axel. The hybrid style of the architecture of the Foscari Tomb is representative of Venetian building ca. 1460.

In painting too the Gothic style lingered on, only gradually supplanted by a Renaissance idiom which Venetian painters learned at Padua. Of crucial importance for the evolution of Paduan painting was Donatello's arrival there in 1443 and his execution of the *Crucified Christ*, the High Altar of the Santo, and the monument of the *Gattamelata*. The revolutionary impact of Donatello's art upon the painters of Squarcione's circle was almost immediately apparent in the frescoes by Niccolò Pizzolo and Andrea Mantegna in the Ovetari Chapel. Between 1448 and 1450 the Venetian painters Antonio Vivarini and Giovanni d'Alemagna also were employed in the Ovetari Chapel, and it is therefore not to be wondered at that the earliest trace in Venetian painting of Mantegna's acerbic linearity occurred in the contribution of Antonio Vivarini's younger brother, Bartolomeo, to the altarpiece which the two brothers executed jointly in 1450 for the Certosa di Bologna. Very likely, the marriage in 1453 of Nicolosia, daughter of Jacopo Bellini, and Mantegna made the latter better known among Venetian painters. His was the decisive influence on the young Giovanni Bellini, and by the 1460s his style dominated Venetian painting. Gentile Bellini was no less indebted to Mantegna than was his brother or Bartolomeo Vivarini. Even Antonio Vivarini eventually succumbed to the influence of Mantegna.

The art of Donatello and Mantegna had no impact on the sculpture of Bartolomeo Bon who, born probably early in the fifteenth century, remained faithful throughout his life to the tenets of a Gothic style. The earliest appearance of Paduan innovations in Venetian sculpture can be traced to the Cenotaph of Federico Cornaro in the Cornaro Chapel, S. Maria dei Frari, probably carved in the mid-1450s.[16] Composed of a life-size angel standing within a tabernacle holding an inscribed scroll, the monument amalgamates the motifs of the small angel in relief with a coat of arms standing within a tabernacle sometimes found in the center of Venetian sarcophagi[17] and the life-size free-standing figure of the deceased within an architecturally independent tabernacle.[18] Francesco Sansovino attributed the cenotaph to an otherwise unknown Jacomo Padovano.[19] Its Paduan provenance is confirmed by the fastening of the cloak of the figure, derived from that of the *Madonna* of the High Altar of the Santo. The proportions, facial type, and drapery of the angel—now transformed into a pagan Victory—resemble those of Donatello's figures in the reliefs of the Santo altar. The prominent inscription carved in Roman uncials, replacing the traditional shield, recalls the classical inscriptions scattered in profusion throughout Mantegna's Eremitani frescoes.[20] Analogous architectural detailing can be found in the throne and lunette of Giovanni da Pisa's altarpiece for the Ovetari Chapel and in the settings of Mantegna's Ovetari frescoes.[21] Indeed, the fresco surrounding the tabernacle has, with justice, been attributed to Mantegna himself.[22] In 1453 Donatello was paid for a *Madonna* installed above the sacristy portal of S. Maria della Carità.[23] Although no trace of it remains, its existence testifies to a wider appreciation of Donatello's art—no longer confined, as in 1438, to the group of Florentines for whom Donatello carved the statue of *St. John the Baptist* in the Frari. Probably from the early 1460s dates the altarpiece in the Miani Chapel in S. Maria dei Frari. In spite of its Gothic partitioning articulated by Gothic forms, its figure types and drapery reflect that degree of the assimilation of Mantegna's art represented by the four Carità altarpieces executed between 1460 and 1471 under Giovanni Bellini. It is within the context of the gradual assimilation of the art of Donatello and Mantegna between 1455 and 1470 and its fusion with traditional Venetian forms and iconography that the works of Niccolò di Giovanni must be seen. He was a major exponent of this trend and, by virtue of his espousal of the values of Donatello and Mantegna, occupies a unique position in the history of Venetian sculpture.

NOTES

1. Andrzé Wyrobisz, "L'attività edilizia a Venezia nel xiv e xv secolo," *Studi veneziani*, vii, 1965, pp. 307ff. In the Senate's second resolution of May 31, 1459, the reasons for the remaking of the census were given thus: "perché algune son invechiade e ruinade, algune per legati e vendede in altri transferide, assaissime da novo reformade e fabricade, e de acque e paludi, orti et terreni vachui in amplissime habitacion et optime possession convertide." (*Ibid.*, p. 310.)

2. Thus claimed Abbot Paruta in his dispute with the mason, Antonio da Cremona, over the construction of S. Gregorio. The dispute took place in January 1461. Earlier prices and wages referred to are those which had obtained at the making of the contract sometime between 1450 and 1455. See Giuseppe Marzemin, "Le abbazie veneziane dei SS. Ilario e Benedetto e di S. Gregorio," pt. 2, *Archivio veneto*, ser. 3, xxiii, pt. 2, 1912, p. 394.

3. On December 22, 1460, the Milanese ambassador at Venice, Antonio Guidobono, wrote to Duke Francesco Sforza at Milan: "Et li mandasse qualche pichaprede de questi da Millano et fare pacto con loro la, ad raxone de tanto el mexe. Et guardariano el lavore et lavorariano. . . . Dicho bene anchora che, quando se vora lavorare meglio, sera mandare de la et maystri de muro et marangoni et lavoratori anchora, perche forsi se avantagiara el terzo de manifactura, perche qua guadagnano molto ingrosso, forsi el dopio, o al mancho el terzo più che non hano de la." On January 4, 1461, Sforza wrote to Guidobono: "et cossi successive provederemo ad quanto sarà bisogno per lavorare, et mandaremo alcuni maystri de qua, là, perchè ne trovamo migliore mercato." On January 26, 1461, the duke's architect, Benedetto Ferrini, wrote from Venice to the ducal secretary, Giovanni Simonetta: "Avisandovi che in questa terra se paghino molto bene li magistri, se paghe el dopio piu de quello se pagaria a Milano." In this letter Ferrini is referring principally to master joiners. For the letters quoted above see Luca Beltrami, *La "Cà del Duca" sul Canal Grande ed altre reminiscenze sforzesche in Venezia* (per nozze Albertini-Giacosa), Milan, 1900, pp. 23, 25, 30, respectively.

4. Agostino Sagredo, *Sulle consorterie delle arti edificative in Venezia*, Venice, 1856, p. 302, no. XLVIII: ". . . adunado questo nostro Capitolo del povero mestier di taiapiera per schivar molti inconvenienti et scandoli intravegnudi et intravegnerano ogni zorno piui per esser el dito mestier nele man de homeni che non sono de le terre de Venetiani ne ad quelli portano amor ne a nisun suo subdito per cason che i diti non stanno ne

vieneno in questa terra cum la suo fameia: L'andarà parte che Damò in avanti: Nesun dela predita arte non possi tegnir botega de taiapiera nè in quella comprar per si ne per altri ne far comprar ad altri per loro salvo se i diti non vieneno a star cum tutte le loro fameie a Venesia et in quella continuo habitar soto pena de lire cinquecento de pizoli per cadauna fiada i serano acusadi. . . ."

5. *Ibid.*, pp. 299f., no. XLIIII: "Et si como a tuti e noto el mistier de taiapiera per el passado soleva esser in gran colmo et molte fameie sì de patroni como de lavoranti viveno de quello, al tempo presente per vegnir di lavori forestieri et fati fuor de Venesia in questa tera compidi: el dito nostro mestier de taiapiera vien de di in di in desolatin et destruction. . . . Per la qual cosa siando el nostro mestier vegnudo a tal conditione e nichilation che se per mezanità de le vostre magnificentie [*Giustizieri vecchi*] non vien sovegnudo e redrezado et obstado che algun lavor fato pertenente al nostro mestier de taiapiera non possa vegnir in questa terra del tutto el dito mestier nostro tanto utele e necessario a questa città el anderà in gran ruina: Et pero landera parte che damò in avanti . . . de alcune parte non se possa condur over far condur in questa terra alcun lavor pertinente al nostro mestier di taiapiera el qual sia lavorado principiado over compido soto pena de perder i lavori conduti fati principiadi over compidi portinente al mestier nostro et de libre trexento de picoli."

6. Giambattista Lorenzi, *Monumenti per servire alla storia del Palazzo Ducale di Venezia*, pt. 1, Venice, 1868, p. 100, doc. 214.

7. On September 27, 1465, the *Giustizieri vecchi* approved a statute proposed by the stonecarvers' guild according to which no stonecutter might undertake to finish a work if the master who began it had not been paid, unless the first master gave his consent. See Sagredo, *op. cit.*, p. 291, no. XXIIII.

8. Giacomo Loredan (d. 1471; four times *Capitano Generale del Mar*) was buried at S. Elena along with his father, Pietro (d. 1439), also a military hero, beneath an elaborately carved tomb slab. Its appearance is preserved by Grevembroch, *Mon. Ven.*, i, p. 57.

9. See Anne Markham Schulz, "The Sculpture of Giovanni and Bartolomeo Bon and Their Workshop," *Transactions of the American Philosophical Society*, in press.

10. See Wolters, 1976, i, pp. 112ff., 266f.

11. Pohlandt, *BJ*, 1971, p. 163, n. 5.

12. See below chapter 2, n. 21.

13. Andrea Moschetti, "Un quadriennio di Pietro Lombardo a Padova (1464–67) con una appendice sulla data di nascita e di morte di Bartolommeo Bellano," *Bollettino del Museo Civico di Padova*, xvi, 1913, pp. 92f., doc. xxii; 93f., doc. xxiii; 96f., doc. xxvi.

14. Erice Rigoni, "Notizie riguardanti Bartolomeo Bellano e altri scultori padovani," Padua. Accademia di scienze lettere ed arti. *Atti e memorie*, n.s. xlix, 1932–33, p. 203.

15. Andrea Moschetti, "Pietro e altri lapidici lombardi a Belluno," Venice. Istituto veneto di scienze, lettere ed arti. *Atti*, lxxxvii, pt. 2, 1927–28, p. 1514, doc. xxvi.

16. For an account of the various dates assigned to the cenotaph see Pincus, 1974, p. 349.

17. See the examples in Turin, Museo Civico (illustrated in Wolters, 1976, ii, fig. 16), and in Prata di Pordenone, S. Giovanni dei Cavalieri, Tomb of Pileo I da Prata (*ibid.*, ii, fig. 52).

18. See the Monument of Enrico Scrovegni, Arena Chapel, Padua (*ibid.*, ii, fig. 35).

19. Sansovino, 1581, p. 66r.

20. Andrea Moschetti, "Le inscrizioni lapidarie romane negli affreschi del Mantegna agli Eremitani," Venice. Istituto veneto di scienze, lettere ed arti. *Atti*, lxxxix, pt. 2, 1929–30, pp. 227–239.

21. Giuseppe Fiocco, "Un affresco di Andrea Mantegna a Venezia," *Dedalo*, vii, 1926–27, p. 536, compared the cornucopias below the tabernacle with those of the crowning of Giovanni da Pisa's altarpiece for the Ovetari Chapel and the frieze of the tabernacle with the almost identical frieze of Donatello's tabernacle for the Parte Guelfa at Or San Michele, Florence. The back of the throne of St. John the Evangelist in a roundel of the Old Sacristy, S. Lorenzo, is identical in form to the Cornaro tabernacle. The tabernacle of the *Cavalcanti Annunciation* in S. Croce is also very similar to it.

22. *Ibid.*, pp. 535ff.; *idem, L'arte di Andrea Mantegna*, Venice, 1959, pp. 115ff.

23. Gino Fogolari, "La chiesa di Santa Maria della Carità di Venezia," *Archivio veneto*, ser. 4, v, 1924, p. 104.

I History and Analysis of the Venetian Works

Probably the earliest in the group of works which forms the object of this inquiry is the monument which stands against the right wall of the choir of S. Maria dei Frari in honor of Doge Francesco Foscari (Fig. 1). On April 15, 1423, Foscari succeeded Doge Tomaso Mocenigo. Under Foscari the west wing of the Ducal Palace, initiated shortly before Mocenigo's death, was finished, the Porta and Porticato della Carta were erected, and the Arco Foscari was commenced. In foreign policy Foscari was responsible for the aggressive course by means of which Venice, allied with Florence against Milan, consolidated its dominion over the terra ferma. The enmity of certain Venetian nobles combined with Foscari's advanced age and poor health brought about the extraordinary measure of his deposition on October 23, 1457. On October 30, 1457, Pasquale Malipiero was chosen to succeed him, and on November 1, 1457, Foscari died at the age of eighty-four. The rapid succession of the doge's deposition and death generated much public sympathy. The *Signoria* also seems to have experienced a change of heart, decreeing for him at public expense the exequies customarily reserved for a reigning doge, over the protests of Foscari's embittered widow.[1] On the night of November 3, Foscari's corpse, dressed in a doge's golden cloak, *berretta*, and golden spurs, with his golden shield at his head, was carried into the Sala del Piovego of the Ducal Palace. There twenty gentlemen dressed in scarlet robes

Left and right are reckoned from the vantage point of the spectator except in analyses of individual statues where left and right refer to a particular part or member of the figure.

9

stood guard. The next day, under a canopy of cloth of gold, his body was carried through the Merceria to the Frari by the principal sailors of Venice, accompanied by the *Signoria*, the clergy, the members of the Venetian *scuole*, the twenty attending gentlemen, nobles and citizens, and the new doge, dressed in the simple raiment of a senator. The funeral oration of four hours was delivered by Bernardo Giustiniani,[2] and the corpse was inhumed in the Frari.[3]

The long inscription beneath the sarcophagus was probably composed by Bernardo Giustiniani.[4] Written in the first person singular, as though by Foscari himself, it lauds the achievements of the doge who studied to emulate the glory of the greatest princes with intelligence, eloquence, memory, justice, fortitude, and resolution. In the course of more than thirty years, it relates, Foscari waged war on land and sea for the safety and dignity of Venice, sustaining the precarious liberty of Italy. He forcibly suppressed the revolts of Brescia, Bergamo, Ravenna, and Crema. He give peace to Venice, uniting Italy in an alliance, and embellished the city with every kind of ornament. There follow his age and date of death and the admonition to preserve justice and concord in order that the dominion of Venice might be eternal.

It has not been noted hitherto that the inscription on the base of the left column contains a dedication, not only to the doge, but also to his grandson, Francesco di Jacopo.[5] At the doge's death, Francesco di Jacopo and his younger brother, Niccolò, both still children, were the doge's only surviving male descendants and were therefore made his residual heirs.[6] We do not know how long Francesco outlived his grandfather: the absence of his name from genealogies of the Foscari family suggests he died in childhood. Niccolò, on the other hand, lived to an advanced age, distinguishing himself in service to the state. It was he who was financially responsible for the erection of the tomb, as the inscription beneath the right-hand column states.[7] Foscari's testament did not specifically charge his heirs with construction of his tomb. But construction of tombs in Renaissance Venice was customarily undertaken by the heirs; exceptions are singularly rare and occurred only when, because there were no male descendants, the tomb's future occupant saw to its construction before he died.

No documents concerning the date of the tomb have come to light. It is first described by Georges Lengherand on March 22, 1486,[8] by which time it must have been finished. By December 11, 1479, when members of the Alberto family were granted the privilege of laying a floor tomb in the middle of the main chapel "tra i sepolcri delli due Prencipi,"[9] space on the right wall of the Cappella Maggiore of the Frari must at least have been ceded for the construction of the tomb. The tomb is generally dated soon after the doge's death,[10] a moment with which its composition—transitional between Gothic and Renaissance[11]— and the style of its individual components accord.

The tomb is surrounded by a poorly preserved fresco representing a wall hanging of gilded leather partitioned by architectural moldings and four medallions containing Foscari arms and the lion of St. Mark.[12] The tomb contains a sarcophagus supported by four consoles (Fig. 1). The front face of the sarcophagus bears half-length female personifications of the theological virtues, *Charity*, *Faith*, and *Hope* (Figs. 5, 6, 9). On the left side of the sarcophagus is a Franciscan saint—either *St. Francis* (without stigmata) or *St. Anthony of Padua*—holding a book (Fig. 8). On the right is *St. Mark* holding a quill and book (Fig. 10). The sarcophagus supports a bier with its funerary cover and pillow in front of which sit two pairs of *putti* with Foscari's coat of arms. The recumbant effigy wears a *bavaro* composed of two rows of ermine skins over a long fur-lined *manto*, the *camauro* and *corno ducale* with a diamond pattern incised on its border, gloves and shoes with pointed tips—the costume in which the doge traditionally appeared in public (Fig. 31).[13] By the effigy's side lies a sheathed sword as it customarily did at the doge's lying-in-state. Female personifications of the cardinal virtues attend the doge: *Fortitude* with her column and *Temperance* mixing wine with water at his feet (Fig. 15); *Prudence* with her mirror at his head (Fig. 16). The figure behind *Prudence*, which ought to represent *Justice*, has no attribute at all (Fig. 16). Above the effigy a baldachin is held apart by two young warriors dressed in armor but otherwise unarmed, who lean on shields bearing Foscari's coat of arms (Figs. 11, 12). These figures stand on a strange array of bases, consoles, and colossal columns resting on high podia by means of which the tomb, located high on the wall, is connected to the ground (Fig. 1). On either side of the *baldacchino*, within effulgent medallions, are Foscari's arms surmounted by the *corno ducale*. The entablature of the tomb, continuous with that of the Cappella Maggiore, divides the human from the divine realm. Below, the mortal remains of the doge are accompanied by the virtues he practiced when alive, an inscription lauding his achievements and symbols of ducal power. Above, the kneeling figures of *Gabriel* and the *Virgin* reenact the announcement of Christ's conception, opening the cycle of events by means of which redemption was effected (Figs. 29, 30). As the most benign and powerful intercessor, the *Virgin* gazes down at the defunct. In the center of the tomb the cycle of redemption terminates with an image of the *Risen Christ* (Fig. 28). *Christ*'s gaze is focused in the high altar where his redeeming sacrifice was reenacted daily at the mass.

The central image of the frontispiece is often misinterpreted as Christ accompanied by the soul of the deceased in the form of a child (Figs. 27, 28, 32). Examination at first hand, however, permits the constatation that what is represented is not a child but a blessing angel whose fluttering garments betoken flight and that there was originally a second angel on the other side of *Christ*. The figure of *Christ* is identical to that on the reverse of all Venetian ducats (Fig. 71), from their earliest coinage decreed on October 31, 1284,[14] until the mid-sixteenth-century reign of Gerolamo Priuli. In both tomb and ducat a standing figure of Christ garbed like ours, holding a book in his left hand and blessing with his right, is contained within a *mandorla* of identical proportions. This image probably derives from scenes of the *Ascension* (Fig. 69) where Christ is frequently represented in this guise and where two angels, like those in the Foscari Tomb, sometimes bear aloft either Christ himself or his *mandorla*.[15] Identical images occasionally occur in scenes of *Christ's Glorification*[16] to signify that Christ was glorified at the moment of his Ascension.[17]

The occurrence of this imagery in a funerary context is unique to the Foscari Tomb: there is no other Italian example known to me.[18] I doubt that the image of *Christ Ascending into Glory* depicts that hope, given concrete form so often in funerary monuments, that the deceased's own soul might ultimately ascend to heaven, for in other tombs it is almost invariably the scene or figure of Christ from the *Resurrection* that is made the bearer of that iconographic message.[19] After Tino da Camaino's introduction of the *Resurrection* in the Tombs of Riccardo Petroni and Gastone della Torre, of 1318 and 1319, respectively, the theme became extremely popular in funerary sculpture, particularly in Venetian Quattrocento tombs. In the Tombs of Doge Niccolò Tron and Doge Pietro Mocenigo a *Resurrected Christ* occupies precisely the position reserved in the Foscari Tomb for the *Ascending Christ*.[20] The traditional preference of *Resurrection* to *Ascension* is justified: whereas the Ascension and Glorification of Christ was a unique event, all virtuous men might aspire to resurrection to an eternal life in heaven at the Second Coming of Christ. (Awareness of the origin of the imagery of the *Ascending Christ* in scenes of the apotheosis of Roman emperors[21] is not likely to have made the interpretation of the *Ascension* as anticipation of elevation to a heavenly abode more acceptable in ducal tombs, for the doge, as merely the most august representative of the Venetian *Signoria*, was not inclined to claim for himself imperial prerogatives.) Rather, I believe that in the Foscari Tomb *Christ Ascending into Glory* stands for the real ruler of Venice whose surrogate the doge was thought to be and to whom his service as sovereign of the state was dedicated, just as it does on the reverse of the Venetian ducat inscribed "SIT · T · XPE · DAT · Q · TV · REGIS · ISTE · DVCAT"[22] —"Let this duchy which thou rulest be dedicated to thee, O Christ." Its unique appearance in this ducal tomb may be explained by the doge's deposition: the *Ascending Christ* implies that, as doge, Foscari was directly responsible to Christ and not to the Venetian *Signoria*.

The form of the Foscari Tomb is dependent on the Tomb of Tomaso Mocenigo of 1423 in SS. Giovanni e Paolo by Pietro Lamberti and Giovanni di Martino da Fiesole.[23] In both, a sarcophagus, supported by consoles, bears a recumbent effigy and three-dimensional attendant figures at its head and feet. This combination of units is enclosed by a *baldacchino* (first introduced into funerary sculpture in Donatello's Tomb of Baldassare Coscia in the Florentine Baptistry) supported by a central tent pole and suspended from an elaborate

Gothic finial which in turn provides a podium for a life-size standing figure. The folds of both canopies descend below the sarcophagus. In both, the plastic, space-enclosing *baldacchino*, which shelters elements of uncompromised volume, contrasts with the wall behind it, treated like a screen. A precedent for the linking of pavement and suspended tomb by means of elongated columns at either side surmounted by sharply projecting consoles exists in the Tomb of Agnese (d. 1410) and Orsola (d. 1411) Venier in SS. Giovanni e Paolo.[24] The reversed capitals which serve the warriors as bases may derive from the bases of the *doccioni* on the west facade of S. Marco.[25] The decoration of the frieze of the Foscari Tomb is very similar to that of the frieze beneath the effigy of Doge Antonio Venier (d. 1400) in SS. Giovanni e Paolo.[26] The location of the *Virtues* on the sarcophagus can be traced in Venice to the Doge Venier Tomb where their disposition parallels that of the Mocenigo Tomb. Half-length personifications of the cardinal virtues were applied a little later to the front face of the sarcophagus of Filippo Cornaro (d. 1410) in S. Pietro di Castello. Funerary *reggistemma* first appeared in 1456 in the frescoed Tomb of Niccolò da Tolentino by Castagno in the Florentine Duomo, but they differ from the *Foscari Pages* in scale, dress, and position. Soldiers of approximately the scale of the effigy, dressed in a manner similar to the *Foscari Pages* and located in comparable positions on independent bases, spread apart the curtains of a large tent in the equestrian monuments of Cortesia Sarego erected between 1424 and 1429 in S. Anastasia, Verona, and Spinetta Malaspina from S. Giovanni in Sacco, Verona, now in the Victoria and Albert Museum. But these warriors, placed within the tent, do not bear the defunct's coat of arms: the use of soldiers as shield bearers seems to be an innovation of the Foscari Tomb.

The Foscari Tomb is made of a limestone probably quarried in the Vicentine. Sabellico twice remarked upon its gilding.[27] Traces of it still visible today suggest that originally the tomb was gilded nearly in its entirety and that the blue background of the half-length *Virtues* and lining of the cloak of the left-hand *Warrior*, the red on his shield, as well as the oxidized paint which has turned the flesh of all the figures black, are later restorations. Considerable damage to the tomb appears to have been incurred in the course of installation. In order to fit the *Effigy* and four *Virtues* on the sarcophagus, the rear corner of the cushion underneath the doge's head; his inner foot, ankle, and surrounding drapery; the inner left-hand corner of the bier; and the entire left hand and bottom of the object held by the so-called *Justice* were broken off. A piece of drapery behind the foot of *Fortitude* is missing. The *Effigy*'s right hand, *Gabriel*'s right hand, and both hands of *Christ*'s companion are more or less severely damaged. The disappearance of the second angel makes visible the crude hacking of the left side of *Christ*'s drapery and the rough excavation of the left side of his base where the *Angel*'s base was originally inserted. Portions of the *mandorla*, rays, and drapery that were overlapped by the *Angel* show no traces of painting or gilding. It is not possible to date the disappearance of the *Angel*. We know only that it was already missing when the tomb was engraved in 1777 by Marco Sebastiano Giampiccoli.[28]

On the basis of the caption to Giampiccoli's engraving the tomb is generally attributed to Antonio Bregno, sometimes with the assistance of his putative brother, the architect Paolo Bregno. At a certain point the name of Bregno was confused with that of Rizzo. Mariacher recently proposed that Bregno was assisted by the young Antonio Rizzo. No other authors have been suggested for the tomb.[29]

The unprecedented conception of its figures makes the Foscari monument almost unique among Italian Renaissance tombs: Pygmalion-like, our sculptor has brought statues to life. This appearance of life is not to be confused with realism, for only in their enlarged scale—nearly equal to that of the life-size *Effigy* itself—and in their unabridged three-dimensionality (the majority of the figures are free-standing and are carved in their entirety)—are the Foscari figures more realistic than the figures on most preceding tombs. Indeed, their original gilding must have made them seem less real. Rather, their appearance of life is due in large measure to their independence from the architectural constraints imposed by the structure of the tomb. No figure is placed within the factitious and unnaturally constricted environment of a niche or tabernacle where each figure would be as isolated from the others as on the separate panels of a polyptych. Rather, *Cardinal Virtues* and *Effigy* are assembled, as in a *Sacra Conversazione*, within a single stagelike space defined by a realistically scaled *baldacchino* and a broad sarcophagus deep enough to accommodate five unforeshortened figures. The *Virtues* are not posed frontally or organized serially on a uniform frontal plane —an organization which would have favored a clearer exposition of their meaning. Instead, they are turned sideways and densely overlapped. Other figures are given no more of a setting than a base and possibly a background whose main architectural lines they break. The disposition of figures beneath the *baldacchino* may well have been inspired by Donatello's revolutionary High Altar of the Santo where independent free-standing nearly life-size figures enclosed by a real and spacious architecture were grouped naturally around the enthroned *Madonna*.

But in even larger measure it is the effect of momentary movement—movement which may be theatrically unrealistic like that of Donatello's figures from the Santo reliefs—that brings the statues of the Foscari Tomb to life. Attitudes of *Virtues* and *Warriors* present instantaneous shifts of weight from one foot to the other (Figs. 11, 12, 15, 16). The poses of these figures have no purpose beyond animating the tomb, generating an excitement which is reenforced by Donatellesque convolutions of long, abundant drapery warranted by no known mode of dress. *Prudence*'s mirror is about to fall from her hand; *Temperance*'s water is captured in the midst of flowing from one vessel to another. Heads are turned, gazes are focused, mouths are opened as if in speaking. The figures do not lament. Yet expressions are uniformly grave—almost sorrowful—as though the actors were aware of the sad occasion of their gathering. Thus endowed with life, the figures are no longer subservient to their symbolic meaning. The attribute of *Fortitude* intensifies the drama of her pose; that of *Prudence* is incidental to her movement; that of *Justice* is lacking altogether. Metamorphosed into persons, the *Virtues* have ceased functioning as personifications.

Remarkable also is the freedom with which the figures have been carved—a freedom that betrays the habits of a sculptor accustomed to modeling in wax. In the *Annunciate Virgin* (Fig. 30) the original shape of the block of stone, apparent in the figure's base, had no effect upon the composition of the figure. The knees and feet of the figure are more or less aligned with the four faces of the block, but the figure's upper torso cuts across one corner, while the movement of head and arms skews the figure even further. Thus a single view, whether from the front or sides, penetrates the block of stone's entire depth. Contours are often broken by free-standing forms that project far beyond the remainder of the contour. Limbs and swathes of drapery are frequently carved in the round or are made to seem so by extensive undercutting. Interstices between free-standing elements and their immediate backdrops are often sufficient to permit oblique views to more distant planes. The *Virgin*'s headdress hangs free on both sides of her face. Her right arm is carved in the round, and behind it the stone is excavated to the rearmost limit of the block. Even details, like fingers, not only are carved in the round but are separated by a wide interval from the background of folds. Such extreme dislocations of the surface of the statue multiply and intensify contrasts of light and shadow. Where the surface does not serve as foil for a form placed far in front of it, it is deeply gouged. Trenches separate folds and locks. The crook of a knee or elbow, the sudden change in direction of a piece of cloth, provide occasions for the excavation of a well.

Principles which determined the design of individual elements are evident in the composition of larger units. The *Virgin*, *Gabriel* (Figs. 29, 30), and the four *Cardinal Virtues* (Figs. 15, 16) are unconventionally presented from one side. The lateral view of the human figure is the one which exploits depth most: foreshortened forms lead the eye back past receding planes marked by the attendant overlapping of limbs and folds. Overlapped and foreshortened forms ordinarily yield only partial knowledge: thorough acquaintance demands views from several diverse angles. But the disposition of the figures hardly permits this, and in order to mitigate the natural desire of the spectator to circumambulate the statues the sculptor extended arms and drapery to either side beyond the boundaries of overlapping forms so that no essential portion of a figure is concealed and drapery patterns are never abruptly truncated. Where a figure, such as the left-hand *Warrior* (Fig. 11), is viewed frontally, the pose of the lithe figure is as open as it can be. The drapery of the cloak hangs free in front and back. Every form is undercut: the border of the cuirass stands forward of the lappets, and the smoothly curving contour is broken by the undercutting of the skirts.

The drapery too seems modeled rather than carved. Characteristic of this sculptor are the long swathes of densely gathered bulky folds wound about entire figures. The swathes seem as if made from ribbons of clay, rolled out, then looped around the figures, producing very variable patterns, but ones constituted fundamentally of curves. The curves may be long, conform to arcs, and envelop large portions of the figure. Or they may make a swing, turning into horizontal S's. Sometimes a portion of an arc is stretched out into a straight line. Sometimes a sudden deviation in the path of a swathe—generally toward the outer contour of the figure—introduces a large angle of not quite 90 degrees, as in the drapery over the right thigh of *Christ* (Fig. 28), below the waist of *Prudence* (Fig. 16), and twice at the right elbow of *Charity* (Fig. 5). Swathes may revolve around a form suggesting the continuation of its volume beyond the visible boundary of its silhouette. But more often, they suddenly descend at the outer edges of the figure, furnishing it with a closed outline. In some cases swathes do both, as along *Christ*'s right contour (Fig. 27). Between these swathes the drapery adheres to the body. The oval contours of these "wet" patches are never quite closed. In spite of their adherence, their surfaces are rarely smooth. Here and there low ridges rise and quickly vanish as though a soft substance had responded to slight pressures of a thumb. Even the surfaces of the swathes seem pinched and pressed. Long, deep, abruptly ending grooves gouge their surfaces as if dug by the nail of an index finger drawn along their length. Drapery is embellished by additive bunches—knots and knobs— not by the incisions, facets, and drill holes made with carvers' tools.

This drapery style is similar to that in paintings by Andrea Mantegna datable to the 1450s. Parallels can be drawn, for instance, between the *Foscari Christ* and Mantegna's *Virgin* from the *Assumption of the Virgin* in the Ovetari Chapel, or better still, with his *Resurrected Christ* at Tours from the predella of the S. Zeno Altarpiece (Figs. 28, 68).[30] Here the swathe of drapery which crosses Christ's abdomen and the sequence of folds on his engaged leg are those of the *Foscari Ascending Christ*. Neither work is precisely dated, and we therefore do not know which preceded which. From the unusually graphic quality of the drapery of the *Foscari Christ*, however, I suspect that the giver was Mantegna.

The style of the Foscari Tomb is unitary, indicating the closest supervision by the master in all the stages of the tomb's design and execution. Indeed, the intervention of an assistant can be deduced, not from any change in style, but only from a slight decline in quality. Comparison with *Justice* and *Prudence* (Figs. 16, 18) shows *Temperance* and the front of *Fortitude* (Fig. 15)—that is, her torso, face, and inner arm—to be the work of an assistant. In the latter figures the curves of swathes of folds lack our master's impulsive generosity. The breasts of the figures are less plastically formed. Their hands are inorganically constructed, and their gestures lack the mannered grace of *Prudence* and *Justice*. The surface of *Fortitude*'s torso does not manifest the multiple layering, the bold gouging and under-cutting of *Prudence*'s torso, nor are the folds organized according to any unifying pattern. All doubt of an assistant's participation vanishes before a comparison of the heads of all the *Virtues* (Figs. 19–22). Hair does not grow organically from the heads of *Temperance* and *Fortitude*. Channels between locks pursue a regular and even course, which deprives them of the vivacious, wilful movement of the locks of *Justice* and *Prudence*. The faces are less subtly articulated, and the proportions characteristic of our artist's female facial type, with an extremely high and broad rectangular forehead and tiny pointed chin, have been altered slightly.

The face of *Fortitude* (Fig. 22), however, recurs in the *Warrior* on the right (Fig. 14), which proves, by comparison with that of its mate (Fig. 13), to be of equal mediocrity. The transformation of contours into long continuous curves is visible in the cloak of the right-hand *Warrior* (Fig. 12) and in the unnatural bowing of his free leg. The contrapposto of the *Warrior* on the left (Fig. 11), however imperfectly understood, becomes, in the *Warrior* on the right, a sway in which no distinction is made between the level of engaged and free knees. The slight twist in space of the *Warrior* on the left contrasts with the absolute planarity of the pose of the right-hand *Warrior* whose upper body, from pelvis thrust forward to receding shoulders, is tilted rather than turned. His pose recalls the backward tilt of *Fortitude* which caused her contrapposto, established by the master through a firmly planted leg, to degenerate into a sway (Fig. 15).

The angel *Gabriel* also presents a curiously unsatisfactory appearance (Fig. 29). The figure seems to have been begun on a scale different from that on which it was finished: forms below the figure's waist are larger and more plastic than they are above, while the scale of the head lies somewhere in between. The bent arm of the figure is too thin and short. A front view of *Gabriel* reveals that the bent leg was meant to connect with the hip far above the present hip joint. The angel, moreover, is no more than half a figure; more of its unfinished rear is visible than in the *Virgin*. But the figure's face (Fig. 25) and lowered hand and the drapery of its skirt leave no doubt of the master's authorship. The statue's deformities can be explained only by the exigencies of the block from which he worked—probably a block from which a different figure had already been partly carved. If that preexistent figure were one destined for the tomb, it could only have been *Prudence* (Fig. 18), which, facing in the opposite direction, could have been cut from the rear of *Gabriel*'s block. Then *Gabriel*'s bent leg would correspond to the rear face of the leg of an initial *Prudence*. Since the leg is somewhat smaller in scale than the present leg of *Prudence*, we can surmise that the first version of the figure—if it ever existed—was rejected because it proved too small. In that case, it must have been the first *Virtue* to have been started. However that may be, it is likely that all but the bent leg of the initial figure was obliterated, that the block was turned around and *Gabriel* was then carved from the back of it. The inorganic lateral tilt of the angel's head suggests that it was excavated from the chest and shoulders of a preexistent figure. This, plus the necessity of adapting the scale of the later leg to that of the earlier one, accounts for the diminutive proportions of the torso.

Analogies between the design and architectural detailing of the Foscari Tomb (Fig. 1) and the crowning of the Arco Foscari in the courtyard of the Ducal Palace (Fig. 2) have frequently been noted.[31] The profiles of the roof of the Arco Foscari and the frontispiece of the tomb are identical. The uppermost row of luxuriant acanthus leaves and gigantic beads which ornament the finial supporting the *Ascending Christ* recur in the finial-shaped pedestal of *St. Mark* at the summit. Heads emerging from acanthus leaves occupy the upper friezes of both monuments, and in both, scallop-shell medallions contain a shield surmounted by the *corno ducale* which together fill their height completely. The scale and poses of the *putti* flanking the discs with Foscari's arms are those of the *putti* flanking spheres on the subsidiary pinnacles of the Arco Foscari. Typical of both monuments is the schematism, flatness, and linearity of the ornament. Individual fields are invariably circumscribed by numerous low and finely incised moldings. The background of the friezes is never quite hidden by acanthus leaves. Contrasts of light and shadow are minimized by the low relief of foliage and heads and by the shallow excavation of the roundels. In the Arco Foscari this style is confined to the area of the second story above the narrow corbeled frieze of heads emerging from flamboyant Gothic leafage. That frieze, as well as the architectural ornament below it, by contrast, are characterized by the sharpest possible alternations of light and shadow. The frieze, supported by narrowly spaced consoles, projects considerably. Its ornament is practically free-standing; masses are so densely concentrated that no ground is visible. The frieze is bounded above and below by sharply cantilevered cornices. Below, whole columns occupy the corners of the lateral towers causing bases and entablatures to project. A massy twisted cable—stretched out where used as colonettes, compressed where used as a segmental arch—surrounds the recess of the central pavilion. The plastic Gothic cable moldings of the lower medallions contrast with the planar classical framing of the upper ones. Akin to the chiaroscuro of the lower portion of the Arco is its Gothic colorism—a result of the use of several varieties of stone. By contrast, the crowning of the Arco is uniformly white.

So radical a change in style is best accounted for by the hypothesis of a change in *proto-maestri*.[32] Who could have replaced whom and when could the change have taken place? Unfortunately, the history of the construction of the Arco Foscari is very fragmentary: documents shed but little light. The Arco could not have been begun before January 28, 1438, when Stefano Bon Cremonese was commissioned to erect four of the six bays of the Porticato della Carta, the corridor leading from the Porta della Carta to the Arco Foscari.[33] Gallo reasoned that these bays must be the four at the *cortile*, or east, end of the passage, for the contract of November 10, 1438, with Giovanni and Bartolomeo Bon for the construction of the Porta della Carta at the opposite end of the passageway presupposes an existent fabric to which the portal was to be attached.[34] But nine and a half months is not too short a time for the construction of at least the first of these bays. Therefore Stefano Bon could just as well have begun construction at the west end of the corridor. Various constructions on the terrace above the Porticato della Carta, including the flying buttress, may be related to decisions to reenforce the southern external wall of the Basilica of S. Marco. On May 23, 1454, the Senate ordered the Ufficio del Sal to disburse a monthly sum for the repair and fortification of the basilica "ab ista parte Palatii et Curiae." On February 1, 1472, the Senate moved that the Ufficio del Sal reenforce the exterior of the church by building an arch from the church to the "palatium novum."[35] Two other documents which have been connected with the construction of the Arco Foscari (that of September 10, 1462, which mentions the carving of new columns next to the Basilica of S. Marco,[36] and that of September 6, 1463, which speaks of figures and many other worthy works executed for the Ducal Palace[37]) may or may not concern the structure. In any case, they are not sufficiently specific to be used as evidence for its dating. In his *Res Venetae* published on May 21, 1487, Marc'Antonio Sabellico wrote that the inner entrance of the Ducal Palace, "begun during the principate of Pasquale Malipiero [1457–62], was carried up to the summit under [Doge Cristoforo Moro (1462–71)]."[38] Yet a document of February 25, 1483, discloses that Antonio Rizzo was expecting delivery of stone from Parenzo for the "porta del Palazzo."[39]

The coats of arms which ornament the Arco Foscari are more informative than documents. The arms of Doge Foscari (1423–57) appear twice on the east face of the structure opposite the Scala dei Giganti, in the spandrels of the ground-floor arch. On the same face, the arms of Doge Cristoforo Moro appear twice in the spandrels of the second-floor arch, once above the entrance to the staircase located at the north end of the balcony, twice on the base of the central pinnacle, and once in the shield supported by the *Warrior* standing on the pinnacle at the northeast corner. Moro's kneeling figure appeared originally within the second-story arch, resting on the cornice over the entrance to the balcony. The arms of Doge Niccolò Tron (1471–73) are found in the right spandrel of an arch located at the western end of the terrace above the Porticato della Carta. Opposite this arch, at the eastern end of the terrace, is a door which gives access to the room beyond the balcony of the Arco Foscari. Above its portal are Mocenigo arms. On the south side of the fabric Mocenigo arms appear twice in the spandrel of the arch of the second story, and once on the shield of the *Warrior* standing on the pinnacle at the southwest corner. These arms could refer to either Pietro Mocenigo (1474–76) or Giovanni Mocenigo (1478–85) or both. A statue of one or the other Mocenigo kneeling before the lion of St. Mark was originally located above the lunette of the second story of the south face of the Arco Foscari.

The change in style of architectural detailing analyzed above runs through an area of the

Arco Foscari to which four coats of arms of Doge Cristoforo Moro are prominently affixed. The succession of *protomaestri*, therefore, must have taken place between 1462 and 1471. The style of the lower portion of the Arco accords with what we know of the architecture of Bartolomeo Bon, to whom the Arco is generally attributed. Bon made his testament on August 8, 1464, and probably died soon afterward. I believe he was succeeded at the Arco Foscari by the author of the doge's tomb.

It has been observed that the figure of *St. Mark* at the summit of the Arco Foscari (Fig. 35) derives from the *Ascending Christ* of the Foscari Tomb (Fig. 28).[40] The gesture of *Christ's* blessing hand was adopted for *St. Mark*. From the *Ascending Christ* come the pattern of oval patches of adhering cloth bordered by swathes of undercut and swinging folds, the swag which crosses both ankles as though the feet were bound together, and the densely gathered folds which fall beneath it to the ankles. In both, the legs are set against wings of descending folds. The thick-soled sandals worn by both appear to be similarly fashioned. These analogies suffice to demonstrate the origin of the two works in a single shop. Yet the different facial types and hair, the stocky proportions of *St. Mark*, and the strapwork of his folds prove that the same artist was not responsible for both.

The *Warrior* supporting a shield with a Gorgon's head on the south pinnacle of the east face of the Arco Foscari (Fig. 36) has also been linked with the Foscari Tomb.[41] From the right-hand *Warrior* of the Foscari Tomb (Fig. 12) come the figure's dress, the draping of his cloak, and, to a lesser extent, his pose. Donatello's *St. George* from Or San Michele provided the model for the figure's head. His bowed arm and grasp of the banner, now missing, was copied from his companion on the opposite tower of the east face (Fig. 38). Comparison with this figure makes manifest the *Gorgon Warrior*'s inferior quality, justifying attribution to an assistant whose work we have not yet encountered.

The *Gorgon Warrior*'s mate on the north pinnacle of the east face of the Arco supports a shield with Doge Moro's coat of arms (Figs. 38, 39).[42] Like the *Gorgon Warrior*, the *Moro Warrior* holds in his right hand a short cylinder in the center of which is drilled a round hole, intended for a narrow iron rod. Very likely both *Warriors* originally held the *vexillum Sancti Marci*. The conjunction of ducal arms and the banner of St. Mark corresponds in meaning to the image of the doge with *vexillum* kneeling before the lion of St. Mark: it signifies receipt of the doge's power from the patron saint of Venice.[43] The *Moro Warrior* wears armor and a helmet but his legs are bare and his feet unshod. His skin-tight cuirass, salient and undercut, and the double row of pointed lappets which emerge from underneath it, derive from the left-hand *Warrior* of the Foscari Tomb (Fig. 11). So too does the figure's cloak which, falling to the ground behind the figure, provides it with a backdrop and support.

The difference between the *Moro* and *Foscari Warriors* bespeaks a rapid development.

The proportions of the *Moro Warrior* are less elongated and attenuated. His pose is now not only anatomically and mechanically correct, but it has become the bearer of a dramatic message. The contrapposto of the figure is orthodox in its opposition of engaged leg and relaxed arm, free leg and tensed arm, and in its orientation of divergent axes of hips and shoulders. But as though the possibility of rendering motion had just now been introduced to sculpture, the pose of the *Moro Warrior* is hardly more advanced than that of the immobile Greek archaic *kouros*. The right hip is thrust out very little; axes of hips and shoulders are nearly horizontal; the knee of the free leg is hardly bent and the free foot is planted flatly on the ground; the contrapposto is not accompanied by the slightest turning of the figure. Thus the contrapposto comes to signify less a normal state of relaxation and repose than an abnormally tense readiness to act. Eventual movement of the legs will not first require that the major portion of the body's weight be raised from the engaged leg and thrust-out hip. Already the *Warrior*'s center of gravity has been drawn into his upper torso, as his contracted abdomen, expanded thorax, and raised shoulders indicate. The head and upper torso of the figure are inclined forward slightly as though the *Warrior* were poised to advance. The muscles of his neck are taut; his head is turned; his eyes gaze with fixed intensity. The figure's mouth is opened, not to show that he is speaking, but rather as a sign of rapt concentration on an object outside himself. The tendons of his engaged knee are so tightly knit and the muscle of his engaged thigh so sharply contracted that his tension seems an involuntary response. His engaged arm, bent in so taut and uncomfortable a position and his hand, grasping the banner, betray a deliberate effort which cannot be sustained for long. Yet movement is so slight and weights and forces are so precisely balanced that no instability or transitoriness transpires from the pose.

Nonetheless the treatment of the drapery produces the effect of a transitory state, as it does in the *Virtues* of the Foscari Tomb. A gentle wind ruffles the sheer material of the *Warrior*'s skirt. The rising, sweeping, unsupported folds of the figure's cloak are caught at the midpoint of some continuous motion. As in the drapery of the Foscari figures, hollows are deeply gouged and layers of folds are undercut so that forms are consistently separated by intervals of space.

Music, at the southeast corner of the Arco Foscari (Fig. 40),[44] and her companion on the south face, *Rhetoric* (Fig. 41),[45] have long been connected with the master of the Foscari Tomb. The proportions of the figures, their tiny heads set on preternaturally long necks, recall the *Virtues* in relief from the Foscari Tomb (Figs. 5, 6, 9). The narrow shoulders, attenuated torso, and elongated legs reflect the canon of the lanky *Foscari Warrior* (Fig. 11). The facial type of *Music* is an amalgam of that of *Justice*, *Faith*, and *Charity* (Figs. 19, 4, 3) without precisely imitating any one. *Music*'s forehead is immensely high and protuberant. Her receding hairline, exposed temples, and locks which flow straight back create an extraordinarily broad forehead. The rapidly undulating horizontal locks, the two tiny locks which part at the summit of the forehead, and the locks which, straddling the part at the summit of the crown, form a sort of bow, recur in *Justice*. The high brows indicated by the termination of a fleshy protuberance above the upper lid are those of *Faith*. As in all three Foscari figures, *Music*'s eyes are very small and located very far apart. They are hardly recessed beneath the brow and the eyeballs, covered by a heavy fleshy upper lid like *Justice*'s, are moderately bulbous. The bridge of the thin nose is extremely pinched; its tip is small but spherical and salient like the noses of *Faith* and *Charity*. The small mouth, with its slightly parted lips, reappears in *Justice*. In both, the lower lip is fuller, more protuberant, yet less definite than the slightly constricted upper lip. In neither do upper or lower lips reach the corners of a mouth demarcated by tiny oblique folds. In all four faces the broad but short blunt chin is pressed back against the neck, producing an incipient double chin.

The mannered elegance of *Rhetoric*'s left hand (Fig. 41) recalls the hands of *Faith* (Fig. 6). Not only are the inorganically upward-curving thumbs elongated and attenuated, but they do not vary in their width throughout their length. The same highly decorative V separates the thumb and nearly straight index finger of the two left hands.

The drapery of *Music*'s engaged leg (Fig. 40) develops that motif created by Mantegna for his *Resurrected Christ* (Fig. 68) and borrowed in the *Foscari Ascending Christ* (Fig. 28) and *St. Mark* (Fig. 35). The concentric rings outlining *Music*'s breasts repeat a formula found in *Justice* (Fig. 16), while the drapery sweeping across the figure's free foot derives from *Prudence* (Fig. 18).

The group of Doge Moro and the winged lion of St. Mark, which originally crowned the opening of the second story of the Arco Foscari, is known to us only from the mid-eighteenth-century drawing by Johannes Grevembroch (Fig. 34), by which time the banner of St. Mark originally held by the doge had vanished.[46] The group was destroyed in 1797 in accordance with a decree of the revolutionary government established after the fall of the Republic.[47] The kneeling doge, as representative of the Venetian *Signoria*, presses one hand to his breast in an act of homage.[48] The lion rests his paw on the open Gospel, inscribed "PAX TIBI MARCE, EVANGELISTA MEUS"—the greeting which preceded the prophecy by which St. Mark learned that his bones would be redeemed from the infidel at Alexandria and brought to rest on the site at which Venice was later founded.[49] The lion strides across a base which simulates both land and water to symbolize Venetian domination of land and sea.

On the mere basis of the record made by Grevembroch it would be hazardous to asseverate our master's authorship.[50] Nevertheless, I think it likely. Inflected folds which seem considerably more agitated than the stable pose warrants resemble those of the *Effigy of Foscari* (Fig. 31), and the opening of the cloak leaves exposed the same amount of cuff.

Stylistic considerations justify an attribution to our master's shop of the tomb, now dis-membered and in large part destroyed, of Ser Orsato Giustiniani (Figs. 42–47). Procurator of S. Marco in 1459, Giustiniani served as Venetian ambassador on several occasions. In 1463 he was elected *Capitano del Mar* in the wars against the Turks, and was leader when the Venetian navy was defeated at Metelino. His sudden death at Modon on July 11, 1464, followed soon after his defeat. His body was returned to Venice, and a funeral, at which Giovanni Caldiera delivered the oration, was held at SS. Giovanni e Paolo on August 4, 1464.[51] In his testament of June 15, 1462, Giustiniani had ordered his burial in S. Andrea della Certosa.[52] He left 300 ducats to be disbursed by Ser Giovanni da Brazza, steward to the procurators of St. Mark's from 1460 to 1467, for the completion of his tomb. Should that not suffice, Marino Giustiniani, son of Orsato's brother Pancrazio and Orsato's heir,[53] was to contribute what was lacking. Prior to the completion of the tomb, Orsato's body was to repose in a coffin placed within a wooden monument with his coat of arms. Should Giovanni da Brazza die, responsibility for construction of the tomb was to devolve upon the executors of Orsato's testament, the *Procuratori di S. Marco de citra*. It seems that the will, or perhaps only that portion of it concerning the construction of the tomb, was contested. On or be-fore April 22, 1466, the procurators of St. Mark's agreed to give Giovanni da Brazza 300 ducats for the making of the tomb in accordance with a legal sentence relayed to them.[54] On the same day they gave Giovanni 200 ducats as part of the larger sum. On December 1, 1466, they gave him the remaining 100 ducats. The use of the verb "to complete," rather than "to make," in Giustiniani's testamentary charge to Giovanni da Brazza strongly sug-gests that the tomb was, in some measure, begun by June 15, 1462. But it cannot have been finished at the time of the procurators' decision of 1466. Indeed, the sum they were called upon to disburse and the fact that it was said to be destined for the "making of the sepul-chre" indicate that the greater part of the work on the tomb still remained to be done. The inscription on the tomb, recorded by Sanudo and others, stated that the tomb was con-structed for his uncle by Marino Giustiniani.[55] The free-standing marble tomb stood at the center of a richly ornamented funerary chapel erected, probably also by Marino, to house the tomb.[56] The chapel was located in the old church dedicated to SS. Eufemia, Dorothy, Tecla, and Erasma in the minor cloister of the later fifteenth-century church of S. Andrea della Certosa.[57] As a result of the Napoleonic suppression, S. Andrea was con-signed to the army and then demolished. Its ornaments and furnishings were sold.[58]

A drawing of the Giustiniani Tomb was made by Johannes Grevembroch in 1754 (Fig. 47).[59] The drawing shows a parallelepiped sarcophagus with imbricated cover. On it, a low bier with lion paw feet support the effigy in the full-sleeved robe of a senator.[60] Beneath the center of the bier is a winged heart. A sheathed sword rests on the cover of the sarcophagus. The face of the sarcophagus is divided into two compartments in each of which a beribboned garland surrounds a scallop-shell medallion on which is superposed a profile portrait of a Roman emperor. At the corners and in the center, standing on projecting semi-circular bases, are female statuettes personifying virtues.

Though common north of the Alps, free-standing tombs are rare in Italy. Indeed, the Giustiniani Tomb seems to have had no Venetian precedent. It was followed by Paolo Savin's Tomb of Cardinal Zen (d. 1501) in S. Marco. Raised on corbels, an identical sarcophagus with *Virtues* was incorporated into the wall Tomb of Doge Niccolò Tron (d. 1473) in S. Maria dei Frari. The medallions with shell fluting and Roman imperial profile portraits in the wall bench of the Cappella Corner in the Frari may derive from those of the Giustiniani Tomb.[61] The bier of the Giustiniani Tomb with its central wings and its legs of lion's paws from which rinceaux unfurl comes from Desiderio da Settignano's Tomb of Carlo Marsuppini in S. Croce, Florence. The free-standing statuettes on semicircular bases placed catercorner at either end of the sarcophagus and the inclination of the lower level of the bases have been traced to the warriors and their bases at the corners of the sarcophagus in the Tomb of Doge Tomaso Mocenigo.[62]

At the left corner of the tomb stood *Hope*, her hands crossed on her chest, her head in-clined, and her gaze directed upward. Opposite her stood *Charity*, her upraised bowl filled with fruit. In the center, *Prudence* held the severed head of a man. The pose, gesture, and drapery of *Prudence* were probably derived from the beautiful antique draped female figure now in the Museo Civico at Vicenza[63]—undoubtedly the one which served members of the Bon shop on three occasions.[64] In 1926 *Hope* was identified by Planiscig with a marble statuette now in the Metropolitan Museum of Art (Fig. 46). A statuette, now in the Kress Collection, Museum of Art, El Paso, Texas, was identified as *Charity* (Fig. 42). Its head is modern; the fruit is missing from its bowl. A third figure of similar style and identical dimensions and material, standing on the same round base, in the Kress Collection at El Paso, was also recognized by Planiscig as belonging to the tomb (Fig. 43). The figure, which holds a broken vase, probably symbolizes *Temperance*.[65] In 1951 Mariacher found in a private collection in Padua two more statuettes belonging to the group (Figs. 44, 45). They are now owned by the Cassa di Risparmio di Padova e Rovigo. *Fortitude* has a column; her companion lacks an attribute. Both heads are recent restorations. *Fortitude* is missing one lower arm; the other statuette, a hand.[66]

In his *Venetia citta nobilissima* Sansovino attributed the tomb to Antonio Dentone.[67] Although nothing was—or is—known of this sculptor, his name prevailed until the end of the nineteenth century[68] when, on the basis of the similarity between the Giustiniani and Tron sarcophagi first observed by Meyer,[69] Paoletti proposed an attribution to Antonio Rizzo.[70] Paoletti's attribution and its immediate acceptance must be judged in light of the fact that at the time the only statue widely and erroneously regarded as belonging to the tomb was the so-called *Allegorical Figure* now in the Ca' d'Oro, which, in fact, possesses certain Rizzesque qualities.[71] Acquaintance with three of the original figures, however, did not cause Planiscig to revise that attribution, and Rizzo's authorship has received general acclaim, even among those, like Mariacher, who perceived analogies with figures from the Foscari Tomb.[72]

The statuette of *Temperance* (Fig. 43) indiscriminately records motifs already known to us from several sources. Her stance, drapery, and coiffure were borrowed from *Music* on the Arco Foscari (Fig. 40). The hand clutching at the cloak was drawn from that of *Faith* on the Foscari sarcophagus (Fig. 6). Her face (Fig. 50) is analogous to that of *Justice* (Fig. 19). The anonymous *Virtue* in Padua (Fig. 45) is more distantly related to *Rhetoric* (Fig. 41), from which her stance, the gesture of one arm, and the folds which festoon her *Standbein* come. The lowered hand of *Charity* (Fig. 42) derives from that hand of the *Foscari Faith* (Fig. 6), also used for the *Giustiniani Temperance* (Fig. 43).[73]

None of these statues is very good. Not only is it likely that our master delegated the execution of all of them, but he seems to have intervened very little at the stage of their design. The author of *Temperance* (Fig. 43) most closely reflects the style of our master; the author of *Hope* (Fig. 46) does so least. From a knowledge of only three at first hand I hesitate to comment on their authorship: possibly each was carved by a different assistant.

The Tomb of Vittore Capello which surmounts and surrounds the main portal of S. Elena (Fig. 48) should also be enumerated among this master's works. In 1466 Capello succeeded Giacomo Loredan as commander of the Venetian navy. Capello took Athens but was routed by the Turks at Castello di Patrasso. It was said that he died of despair at his defeat on his ship at Negroponte some eight months later. The epitaph beneath the cornice of the portal of S. Elena informs us that he died on March 13, 1467, at the age of sixty-three.[74] News of his death had reached Venice by April 7, 1467, when a new *Capitano del Mar* was elected.[75] Capello's body was returned to Venice where he was given a solemn funeral.[76] He was buried in S. Elena, probably just inside the entrance to the church where, according to an eighteenth-century description, a slab with Capello's arms was set into the pavement.[77] The patrons of the tomb were Capello's three sons and, doubtlessly, his heirs—Alvise, Paolo, and Andrea. As in the Foscari Tomb, their names appear, not in the epitaph which is confined to eulogizing the deceased, but on the podium of a column.[78] There is no reason to suppose that the tomb was not erected soon after Capello's death.[79] After the suppression of S. Elena the statues were removed to SS. Giovanni e Paolo where they remained until the beginning of the present century when they were reunited with the architecture of the tomb on the exterior of the main portal of S. Aponal.[80] The entire tomb was reconstructed in its original site, probably in 1943.[81]

The portal is flanked by two fluted Corinthian columns standing on high plinths of square plan. On the front of these plinths Capello's arms are carved in relief. An inscription is divided between each of the inner sides of the plinths. In addition to the columns, two consoles ornamented with lions' heads and acanthus support a richly ornamented cornice. Between the consoles is the epitaph. The consoles are flanked by reliefs of shields containing Capello's arms. The center of the cornice, broken forward, serves as base for the Istrian limestone figures of *Capello* and *St. Helen* (Fig. 58). *Capello* kneels, his right hand raised in homage to his breast. He is dressed in armor but is respectfully bareheaded. A sheathed sword hangs from his left hip. *St. Helen* bears no attribute. That the empress once wore a crown we can deduce from her headdress, cut away in order to accommodate it (Figs. 51, 53, 55).[82] (A screw for the attachment of a metal halo was probably added later.) Behind the figures, projecting in front of a veined marble background, is a sarcophagus in high relief. The figures and sarcophagus are contained within a semicircular lunette crowned by a flaming vase. The bottom rear corner of the statue of *St. Helen* was cut away in order to accommodate the platform beneath the supports of the sarcophagus, while an arc was excavated toward the rear of *Capello*'s base in order to accommodate *St. Helen*'s base. The saint's left hand is missing.[83] Her drapery, the index finger of her right hand, her face, and the projecting plates of armor on *Capello*'s knees and elbow have been chipped. The exposed portions of the kneeling figure have been badly worn by rain.

The Capello Tomb is the earliest example known to us of a funerary monument incorporated into the exterior portal of a church.[84] Subsequent Venetian examples include Jacopo Sansovino's Monument to Tommaso Rangone at S. Giuliano, Domenico da Salò's Monument to Vincenzo Capello over the main portal of S. Maria Formosa, and the seventeenth-century sarcophagus of the eleventh-century Doge Domenico Contarini at S. Nicolò di Lido. In none of these—nor, indeed, in any tomb—does the iconography correspond to that of the Capello Tomb.[85] Its nearest relatives are images of the doge kneeling before a standing figure of St. Mark on the obverse of the Venetian ducat. Together, doge and saint hold the *vexillum Sancti Marci*. The coin was inscribed with the doge's name and title and "S. M. VENETI."[86] The image signified the investiture of the doge by the patron saint of Venice. The significance of the Capello Tomb is probably the same: Capello is invested as *Capitano del Mar*—an office which cost him his life as the sarcophagus and epitaph remind us—by the church's patron saint, St. Helen.

The object, now lost, which *Capello* and probably also *St. Helen* originally held in their hands has been the cause of some debate. It cannot have been a sword, since Capello is already wearing one. Nineteenth-century engravings show Capello holding the baton of command[87] which contemporary descriptions often mention. It was probably introduced when the figures were reinstalled in SS. Giovanni e Paolo.[88] In the eighteenth century the figures held a cross: that Grevembroch did not invent it for his illustration of the tomb,[89] as we might suspect, is proven by an approximately contemporary description which specifically mentions it.[90] Munman argues persuasively for the iconographical appropriateness and therefore the originality of the cross: "what better way to glorify a general who had devoted his energies to subduing the heathen Turk than to symbolize his efforts to rescue Christianity in the form of his delivering the Cross to St Helena . . . simultaneously recommending himself to her patronage. In this way he completes, in death, the action in the course of which he died."[91] But neither the cross represented by Grevembroch, nor the cylindrical baton, nor the captain's standard, which has also been proposed, correspond to the remnant of the object which *Capello* holds in his hand (Fig. 57). Consisting of one larger wedge which may only be a strut and another smaller, truncated wedge perpendicular to it, the remnant has so far defied my attempts at definition.

In his guide of 1581 Sansovino gave the Capello Tomb to the author of the Giustiniani Tomb. Besides these two, he knew of no other work by Antonio Dentone.[92] The attribution to Dentone was not disputed until 1893 when an examination of the architecture of the tomb induced Paoletti to assign it to Antonio Rizzo. Evident analogies between *St. Helen* and figures from the Foscari Tomb and Arco Foscari he tentatively explained by the possible collaboration of a second master.[93] Paoletti's hesitant suggestion of collaboration was elaborated by Venturi and Munman who attributed to an assistant the execution of the saint.[94] Nevertheless, Paoletti's ascription of the tomb to Rizzo has gained wide currency.[95] Alternative solutions have focused on Antonio Bregno, favored at one time by Planiscig and Fiocco,[96] and Antonio Dentone, whose name was recently reintroduced by Pohlandt.[97]

In her proportions *St. Helen* (Fig. 58) is comparable to *Rhetoric* and *Music* from the Arco Foscari (Figs. 41, 40). Her legs and lower torso are elongated; her waist is raised; her shoulders are narrow. Her breast is small and circular. Her head is elevated on an unnaturally long neck.

St. Helen's pose (Fig. 58) resembles most the poses of *Rhetoric* and *Prudence* (Figs. 41, 16) in which the contrapposto produces an exaggerated thrust of the engaged hip. The knee of the free leg is bent forward, and the free foot, more than half raised from the ground, is turned sharply outward. But rather than repose, this contrapposto expresses lethargy and thus conveys a message diametrically opposed to the meaning of the movement of the *Moro Warrior* (Fig. 38). Instead of an elevated center of gravity denoted by a contracted abdomen and expanded thorax, the center of gravity of the three female figures drops, prohibiting instant movement. Their upper torsos are retracted, their shoulders are not raised; their breasts fall to the level of their waists; their rib cages sink into their slumping and distended abdomens and hips. The arms of all three figures, supported on their hips, betray no tension, and the hands exert no effort. Heads droop forward slightly but do not turn. Mouths are closed; gazes are transfixed as though, looking inward, the figures were oblivious of the external world.

Patterns of folds, such as the reversed L-shaped fold which hangs free at the crook of the knee, the vertical folds beyond it, and the fold which sweeps downward from the knee across the free foot, recur in *Prudence* (Figs. 58, 18). The oval fold falling obliquely across the abdomen and thigh (Fig. 49) recalls the drapery of *Rhetoric* (Fig. 41) and the *Giustiniani Temperance* (Fig. 43).

The face of *St. Helen* (Figs. 51, 53, 55) is as similar to that of the *Giustiniani Temperance* (Figs. 50, 52, 54) as a work of superior quality can be to a poor imitation of it. The elevated brows, whose springing makes half an ogive, enclose an extraordinarily salient brow and bridge. The flesh swells between the brow and upper lid above the outer portion of the eye. The perfect arc of the upper contour of the upper lid is defined in its entirety by a sharply incised groove. Its juncture at the inner corner of the eye with the sinuous line of lower lid gives to the pointed tear duct an identical configuration. The eyes are placed far apart. The protuberance of the eyeball is accentuated by deep indentations at the inner and outer corners of the eyes. A sharply indented groove defines the lower border of the lower lid. In all these respects *St. Helen*'s eyes are comparable to those of *Justice* (Fig. 19). Common to both is the shape of the opening between the lids of the similarly downcast eyes and the points at which the iris is truncated. In both, the lower lid takes a rapid swing upward toward the outer corner of the eye only to be overlapped by the straighter upper lid. The morphology of *St. Helen*'s mouth recurs in the *Foscari Prudence* (Fig. 20) and *Gabriel* (Fig. 25). In the highly articulated upper lip a sharp dip at the center of the lower contour is succeeded by a rapidly rising curve at either side which, descending very gradually, produces the subtlest of reverse curves. This two-dimensional pattern is accompanied by a fluctuation of the surface in which projections coincide with descending curves, recessions with ascending curves. Considerably before the corners of the mouth the upper lip disappears. The lower lip is fuller and broader than the upper lip and, projecting more, is endowed with a more visible boundary. Like *Prudence* and *Temperance* (Figs. 20, 50, 52, 54), *St. Helen*'s chin is small, nearly circular, and extremely jutting. An incipient double chin is visible in all three profiles.

St. Helen's hand (Fig. 49) belongs to the type exemplified by *Rhetoric* (Fig. 41) in which the curvature of the fingers refutes the existence of a rigid bony structure. The plump and tubular, almost swollen, fingers are constricted at their juncture with the hand. The lower contour of the elongated thumb follows a continuously ascending curve, while the division between thumb and straight index finger runs perilously close to the outer border of the hand.

Beneath those features which characterize as masculine and middle-aged the hand which *Capello* raises to his breast (Fig. 56), one can discern the gesture and morphology of *St. Helen*'s hand. The strangely inorganic flexion of the wrist, the tucking of the fourth finger behind the third, and the curvature of the little finger are common to both. In spite of its diverse gesture, the disposition of the fingers of the lowered hand of the *Ascending Christ* (Fig. 28) is similar to that of *Capello*'s hand. The extraordinary precision and detail with which *Capello*'s armor is executed (Fig. 59), revealing now complete mastery of the tools and techniques of the carver's art, as well as many of the motifs—the rinceaux embellishing *Capello*'s shoulder, the overlapping discs of the lappets underneath, the straps—betray the workmanship of the author of the *Moro Warrior* (Figs. 38, 39). The string of beads beneath *Capello*'s shoulder reappears in an identical position in *Fortitude* from the Giustiniani Tomb (Fig. 44). The winged cherub's head on *Capello*'s breastplate has been traced to Donatello's *Gattamelata*. From that source as well come the expressive realism of *Capello*'s head,[98] and the absence of hat or helmet, ultimately traceable to statues of Roman Emperors in military dress.

A comparison of the head of *Capello* (Figs. 60, 61) with that of the *Effigy of Foscari* (Fig. 24) shows the same degree of generalization in which the delineation of individual folds and wrinkles, of hair and accidental deformations of the surface, yields to the realization of larger forms. The relative lack of detail makes the determination of age difficult: both men seem to be about sixty years of age, though Foscari was actually eighty-four. The squarish shape of the two faces combined with their extraordinary depth endow the massive heads with a nearly cubic form. Yet the edges of the cube are scarcely visible, for the forms recede continuously and silhouettes are formed only at the outer descending edges of the brow and the outer limits of the cheekbone. Indeed, it is remarkable how, in spite of inevitable differences of physiognomy, the two men resemble one another. Common to both is the furrowed concave forehead. The small eyes, though not particularly recessed, are overshadowed by low brows which sag above the inner corners of the eyes. The cheekbones are low, protuberant, and widely spaced, and the broad jaws are heavily jowled. The same folds of flesh descend obliquely from the nose and from the inner corners of the eyes, and a prominent but blunt chin of identical shape is bounded above by a sharply incised groove. For their moral rectitude implied by the serious, almost glum, expression, for their generalized treatment of highly specific features inspired by Roman Republican portraiture, for the cubic massiveness of the head and the plasticity of its individual features, the portraits of *Foscari* and *Capello* are indebted to Donatello's *Gattamelata*.

Many of the same distortions are apparent in the faces of *Capello* and *Foscari*. The farther side of the face is shorter than the nearer side: on the farther side, the distance between nose and mouth and, more noticeably still, the length of the nose, have been contracted so that the axes of eyes and brows, on the one hand, and mouth and chin, on the other, visibly converge. On the farther side of the face the inner corner of the eye is located closer to the nose. The slope of the nose is steeper. Indeed, the entire nose is inclined slightly away from the observer. As a result, the nostril on the far side of the face is compressed.

The purpose of these distortions was to make the central projection of the face overlap, to a greater degree than would ordinarily occur, that portion of the face immediately beyond it and thus accentuate the effects of a three-quarter view. For the sake of a more effective silhouette the frown lines have been displaced toward the farther side of the face.

These distortions would have had no purpose if the view in which *Capello*'s head is now presented to the spectator—that is, in profile view—were the one originally intended. However, other indices—most notably the area left unfinished which would coincide precisely with the rear face of the statue if the statue were turned forward by 45 degrees—prove that *Capello*, like so many of our sculptor's figures, was meant to be seen in three-quarter view. As *Capello* is placed now, all the carving on the front of his farther shoulder and upper arm, executed with as much care as the carving on his nearer arm, is invisible. Subtle distortions in the features of her face (Fig. 51) indicate that *St. Helen* too was meant to be turned forward by 45 degrees. In the appropriate three-quarter view *St. Helen*'s gaze would come to rest in *Capello*'s face instead of shooting past the far side of his head.

The figure of *St. Helen* decisively influenced the three female companions of *Rhetoric* and *Music*, two of whom are visible on the south face of the Arco Foscari (Fig. 37).[99] From *St. Helen* come the stance, the gestures, and the abundant drapery made of a thin, adhering stuff, wrapped more like a sheet than a cloak. Instead of the octagonal bases of the earlier statues—bases which accord with the octagons at the summits of the pinnacles—the three female figures have been given the round base of *St. Helen*. More significantly still, they lack the attributes which would have made them identifiable as personifications of the liberal arts.

While comparable to that of the Giustiniani Tomb (Fig. 47), the classical style of the architecture of the Capello Tomb (Fig. 48) is very different from the crowning of the Arco Foscari (Fig. 2) or the Foscari Tomb (Fig. 1). At the Arco Foscari, our master must have sought to accommodate his design to those portions of the gateway already finished. The differences between the Foscari Tomb and the Giustiniani and Capello Tombs—the latter two probably more or less contemporaneous—can be explained by the interval of a decade separating them, during which the architectural style of our master underwent a rapid transformation. While a transformation of this sort would have been anomalous in Florence, in Venice, where Gothic forms flourished late into the Quattrocento, it was not uncommon for architects to compose in diverse idioms concurrently. Bartolomeo Bon's extraordinarily advanced design for the Ca' del Duca was created at the same time as his Gothic portal for the Madonna dell'Orto, and on the *cortile* side of the east wing of the Ducal Palace Antonio Rizzo set a Gothic loggia on one executed by him in pure Renaissance style.

The statue of *St. Christopher* above the main portal of the Madonna dell'Orto (Figs. 62–65) also warrants attribution to our master. Notwithstanding Mariacher's repeated claims of Matteo Raverti's authorship,[100] the figure is generally given to Bartolomeo Bon.[101] Until recently, support derived uniquely from Francesco Sansovino's attribution.[102] In 1961–62, however, Gallo published documents of commission and payment which confirmed Bartolomeo's participation from 1460 to 1461 in the erection of the portal.[103] Yet the documents do not unequivocally corroborate Bon's authorship of the statue of *St. Christopher*. The portal was not finished at Bartolomeo's death. Documents inform us, not only that it still had to be installed (which was not done until 1483), but that the carved foliage of the gable remained to be executed. The *Annunciate* group in the Victoria and Albert Museum, which Bartolomeo may have intended for the portal of the church, was not finished by him,[104] while the figures which do flank the portal are datable by style to a period subsequent to Bartolomeo's death and rarely figure in the literature among his works. Since payments to Bartolomeo do not designate the work accomplished on the portal, it is possible that at his death—probably in the second half of 1464—the statue of *St. Christopher* had not yet been begun and that our master succeeded to Bon's commission at the Madonna dell'Orto just as I believe he did at the Arco Foscari.

The over life-size group carved from Istrian stone (Fig. 62) shows the bearded saint leaning on a staff of wood as he fords a stream. The base simulates rocks, and wavy lines between his legs stand for water. The saint is barefoot. He has drawn his gown above his knees in order not to get it wet. His sleeves are rolled up, and his mantle, fastened with a circular clasp with a bust-length Roman profile portrait, has been thrown back over his shoulders as though to facilitate his movement. Astride one shoulder sits the *Christ Child* (Figs. 64, 65), clutching a tuft of the saint's hair with one hand, and with the other, steadying a globe surmounted by a cross. The heads of both are turned sharply to the right in the direction of the bridge to the *campo* in front of the Madonna dell'Orto. The statue was recently restored[105] and, apart from its worn surface and minor losses in the raised hand of the saint and the foot of *Christ*, is in good condition.

A comparison of the head of *St. Christopher* (Figs. 63, 64) with the head of the *Warrior* on the left of the Foscari Tomb (Fig. 13) or that of *St. Mark* from the sarcophagus (Fig. 10) reveals a common treatment of the hair unique to this artist. Flocks of hair like wool are piled on top of one another in so additive a manner that they seem fashioned out of clay. The tufts curl slightly. Sometimes an accelerating movement toward their tips introduces a tempered reverse curve. At the center of the head they flop forward in separate layers, covering a good proportion of the brow. Beneath them, more tufts, shorter at the forehead, longer at the crown, flop sideways, swelling the contour of the head, particularly at the level of the temples. Beneath the high crown and forehead the features are compressed into the lower half of the face. Common to all are the deep-set eyes and the swelling, as though produced by a contusion, beneath the outer portion of the brows. Globular in form, the eyeball is deeply indented at inner and outer corners. The short nose, pinched at the bridge, swells slightly to either side and ends in a salient spherical tip. The surface of the nose is relatively broad and flat. Its nostrils are thin and do not flare. The upper lip, like that of *St. Helen* (Fig. 51), consists of two reverse curves which, meeting in the center, cause the contour to dip sharply. As there, descending curves produce projections, ascending curves, recessions. As is characteristic of so many of this master's figures, as well as those of Donatello and Mantegna, the mouth is opened slightly. The gap between the lips is of equal width throughout its length, and the corners of the mouth puncture the skin of the cheeks stretched taut by the parting of the lips. Like the *Foscari Christ* (Fig. 23), the lower lip is fuller and broader than the upper lip. In both, the central arch of its lower contour is made by the groove bounding the prominent but blunt, circular chin. In both, the short tufts of hair sprouting from the chin curl inward with a corkscrew movement, leaving an interstice between them. The accentuated plasticity of the *St. Christopher*, the greater emphasis given important features of the face, the defter combination of a tectonic composition and a calligraphic treatment of the locks, and the pronounced effect of intelligent concentration which the focused gaze produces suggest a dating at some years' remove from the execution of the tomb.

The face of the *Christ Child* (Fig. 65) is comparable to that of the *Angel* in the crowning of the Foscari Tomb (Fig. 33). Common to both is the extremely high, broad forehead which protrudes toward the hairline but is indented above the brows. The fleshy upper brow encases opened eyes nearly triangular in shape. The bulbous eyeball is sharply indented in inner and outer corners. Deep creases not far below the lower lids denote the beginning of the cheeks. The mouth is opened. Neither lip reaches the corners of the mouth which perforate the skin stretched taut. In both, the spheroid cheeks bulge most opposite the mouth. The tiny, yet extremely protuberant, chin is separated from the lower lip by a deep broad trench.

The sheer stuff of *St. Christopher*'s gown (Fig. 62), blown flat against his body or fluttering back and to the sides, thus furnishing a foil to silhouetted limbs, recalls the drapery of *Christ*'s angelic companion (Fig. 32), and even more, the *Giustiniani Fortitude* (Fig. 44). The fastening and draping of the saint's cloak recur in the *Foscari Justice* (Fig. 16), while the diagonal fold crossing his breast repeats a pattern from the *Foscari Fortitude* (Fig. 15). The amplitude of curving folds reminds us of the doge's *Effigy* (Fig. 31).

In its technique, the statue of *St. Christopher* (Fig. 62) is comparable to the left-hand *Warrior* from the Foscari Tomb (Fig. 11). In spite of its frontality, neither figure reflects the plan or elevation of the block from which it came. Within a fundamentally closed silhouette, the mass is perforated and internal outlines are continually broken. The head juts forward sharply. A leg bent forward, an arm bent to the side, are carved entirely in the round. Because of multiple, but only partial, overlappings, forms emerge from every level of depth of the block of stone, and even from a frontal vantage point the eye encompasses and penetrates them all. Elements, such as the gown where it overhangs the cinch, are undercut even where the intervals of space are minuscule. Projecting, open forms establish the possibility of oblique perspectives. Yet, with their closed silhouettes and frontal poses, the figures are clearly intended for a single view *en face*. Moreover, the *Warrior*'s cloak and *St. Christopher*'s cloak, rocks, and water form backdrops parallel to the wall against which the figures stand, thus discouraging us from doing what the wall effectively prevents—namely, walking around the statue. Over the surface of the backdrops, whose depth is measured by limbs bent forward or fields of drapery placed far in front, shadows gather, setting off advancing portions of the figure.

Mariacher remarked a similarity between the *Annunciate Virgin* on the right of the portal and *Music* from the Arco Foscari (Fig. 40).[106] From *Music* come the swathe of drapery traversing the *Virgin*'s left shoulder and the position and draping of her right leg. The clasp of the *Virgin*'s cloak resembles that of *St. Christopher*. Yet neither the quality nor the style of the *Virgin* warrants an attribution to our master. Even his supervision is refuted by the treatment of the cloak beneath the *Virgin*'s book. Although the composition of the figure depends from Bartolomeo Bon's *Virgin* in the Victoria and Albert Museum, the *Virgin* from the portal cannot have been produced in his shop either. Until new evidence is unearthed, its eclectic and modest author must remain anonymous.

In the Venetian church of S. Maria del Giglio is a relief which, in spite of its small size, reveals a style common to the works already analyzed (Figs. 66, 67). It shows St. Jerome meditating over a book[107] in his desert retreat at Chalcis (375 to ca. 377) as he described himself in his famous letter to Eustochium.[108] The saint is seated in a niche hollowed from a cave. He is naked but for a tunic of sackcloth. Though his body does not yet show the effects of fasts and vigils, his face is emaciated and manifests the deep depression into which the saint had fallen. Between his legs rests a staff, and at his feet are the lion and the anomalous cardinal's hat—in St. Jerome's day there were no cardinals—recommended by Giovanni di Andrea da Bologna's *Hieronymianus* of 1346.[109] In a third niche three bound books are placed pell-mell. From a fourth emerges a snarling dragon representative of the wild beasts which Jerome described.[110] The stump of a dead tree in the background, a frequent feature in scenes of *St. Jerome in the Desert*, symbolizes physical death as a precondition of heavenly life attained through ascetic discipline and Christian meditation.[111]

The relief is made of Brać stone.[112] It is rather worn and parts are mutilated. The saint's left arm and the half of the opened book which it supported are missing. The sides and bottom edge of the frame are badly chipped. Damage to the latter has caused the loss of most of the lion's right front paw.

Prior to Planiscig's publication of the relief in 1930 the work attracted little notice.[113] His attribution of it to Pietro Lombardo was met with some reserve.[114] Yugoslav art historians almost invariably attribute the relief to Andrea Aleši or his shop.[115]

Yet our master's hand is manifest in the carving of relief no less than in the execution of free-standing statuary. Repudiating the *schiacciato* relief which just then was gaining popularity in Italy, he worked a block of considerable depth, utilizing every plane of it. Principal objects, typically depicted in foreshortened views, occupy several successive planes: the overlapping arm and leg of St. Jerome, folds of drapery, the staff, the beard enumerate multiple layers of depth. Wherever possible, our master made a limb or attribute free-standing, separating it from its immediate backdrop by a measurable interval of space. Where the exigencies of the material prevented the carving of an object in the round, he undercut it: even the farther silhouette of the saint is surrounded by a narrow trench. Thus every form is isolated in a vacuum whose boundary is often defined by the rim of drapery or rock: the saint, lion, dragon, books inhabit niches; the forward leg of the saint emerges from a tunnel of drapery. Cavities so deeply excavated produce pockets of shadow with which the illumination of advancing forms contrasts. Dappling the surface with paler shadows are the holes of the rotting tree stump, the triangular clefts at the junctures of the rocks, the recessed pages of the books. Such devices evoke a very strong sensation of a very limited recession. In fact, distance extends only to the tree stump immediately beyond the cave. In addition to overlapping and foreshortening visible in the inclined planes of the ground and bank on which the saint is seated, in the cardinal's hat and books, as well as in the animals and saint, an impression of receding space is produced by the gradation of the height of the relief. In general, the height of the relief accords with the relative position of the object represented: the farther arm and leg of the saint are flatter than the nearer arm and leg and, unlike them, are attached throughout to the ground, while the tree stump is portrayed in the flattest, though not *schiacciato*, relief. It is only where projecting forms come forward to what must have been the foremost limit of the block of stone, as in the heads of lion and dragon—pressed as though against a window pane—or where the drama of the scene demands a certain emphasis, as in the head of the saint carved nearly in the round, that a certain inconsistency ensues.

In spite of the fact that the type was iconographically inappropriate to the hermit saint, St. Jerome's proportions and physique agree with the giant *Christopher*'s (Figs. 67, 62). Both figures are robust and muscular, with massive shoulders and disproportionately large hands. The legs of the two saints—remarkably similar in spite of the great diversity of scale—possess protuberant and very knobby knees and slightly bowed and extremely prominent shin bones. Bulging calves produce identical outer contours in both right legs. Although Jerome's physiognomy differs from that of *St. Christopher* (Figs. 67, 63), both possess an extraordinarily high forehead and elevated crown. An indentation which spans the entire width of the forehead just above the eyebrows is succeeded by a marked protuberance of equal length. The low straight brows overshadow deeply recessed eyes set far apart. Prominent cheekbones are pushed to the borders of the face.

While St. Jerome's drapery (Figs. 66, 67) has no precise analogy, the type and rhythm of its folds, the isolated patches where the cloth adheres, bounded by swathes which swing across the body from receding shoulder to projecting hip and loop around the limbs, recall the drapery of *Prudence* (Fig. 16), *Rhetoric* (Fig. 41), and most of all, of *Music* (Fig. 40). As there, one contour of each flat and sharp-edged fold is undercut. In both, there is a preference for pairs of parallel folds set at a certain distance from one another. Folds do not run into or around the outer edges of the figure but rather change direction toward its perimeter, following its contour for a certain distance before disappearing. Narrow wings of drapery endow a portion of both figures with a closed and smoothly curving outline. Even the rocks have been given the embracing contours which our master habitually employed for drapery: the curve of the niche enclosing St. Jerome is virtually identical to that of the cloak encircling the arms of *Charity* from the Tomb of Francesco Foscari (Fig. 5).

Simplified in its translation to the medium of relief, the setting nonetheless recalls the landscapes of Mantegna's paintings—of his *Agony in the Garden* in the National Gallery, London, for example, or his *Resurrection* at Tours (Fig. 68). No soil and hardly any vegetation mitigate the hardness of the petrous setting. Rocks are similarly faceted and fissured, and crevices between them similarly imperil the equilibrium of the pile. As in the *St. Jerome*, Mantegna, too, made of the opening of a cave a niche for his protagonist. The large curves controlling the design of St. Jerome's grotto are precisely analogous to the pattern of swirls to which Mantegna's landscapes invariably conform.

In part, the sequence of the works attributed to our master can be determined. A certain awkwardness in the execution of figures from the Foscari Tomb and a technique better suited to wax than stone confirm what the doge's death in 1457 implies—that the Foscari Tomb is the earliest of our master's Venetian works.[116] The influence of the relief of *St. Jerome*, a copy of it, or its prototype, is evident in a work executed between 1470 and 1472. The deft use of carver's drills, points, and chisels which accentuates, rather than camouflages, the natural properties of stone places the relief closer to the end than to the beginning of our master's Venetian sojourn. Among the latest of the Venetian works is the Tomb of Vittore Capello, erected after the captain's death in March 1467. The execution of the Giustiniani Tomb may postdate the Capello Tomb even though Giustiniani died in 1464. In any case, the Giustiniani Tomb cannot have been finished in April 1466 when, after litigation, Giovanni da Brazza received the first installment of money destined for the tomb. The facts that none of the surviving figures was executed by the master and that one does not even show his influence, unlike the other monuments so far considered—evidently autograph almost in their entirety—suggest that it was executed when the master was no longer present. *Music* and *Rhetoric* must predate the *Giustiniani Temperance* and *Virtue* in Padua which they respectively inspired. They, as well as the other figures from the Arco Foscari and the statue of *St. Christopher*, are not likely to precede the death of Bartolomeo Bon probably toward the end of 1464. As we shall see, external evidence indicates that the figures from the Arco Foscari and *St. Christopher* were finished by 1467 and that the Capello Tomb was completed in 1468. But since that evidence is derived from the biography of our master, we must first proceed to proof of his identity.

NOTES

1. For the death and funeral of Doge Foscari see Francesco Berlan, *I due Foscari, memorie storico-critiche*, Turin, 1852, pp. 168ff. For doges' funerals in general see Marino Sanuto, *Cronachetta*, ed. Rinaldo Fulin (per nozze Papadopoli-Hellenbach), Venice, 1880, pp. 79ff.

2. Published in *Orazioni, elogi e vite scritte da letterati veneti patrizi in lode di dogi ed altri illustri soggetti*, Venice, ²1798, i, pp. 21–59.

3. I do not know why the Frari was chosen as Foscari's place of burial instead of SS. Giovanni e Paolo, the most popular site for ducal tombs, unless it reflected a deliberate dissociation from earlier state traditions. Most exceptionally, Foscari made no provision for his burial in his testament of October 29, 1457. (See below, n. 6.) The newly erected Palazzo Foscari was not located in the parish of the Frari, but in that of S. Barnaba. (Crescentino Greppi, "Le case degli Sforza a Venezia e Fra Simone da Camerino," *Archivio veneto*, series 3, xxvi, pt. 2, 1913, p. 330.) Possibly other immediate members of the family had been buried in the Frari. Of this, however, no record survives.

4. "ACCIPITE CIVES FRANCISCI FOSCARI VESTRI DVCIS IMAGINEM. / INGENIO MEMORIA ELOQVENTIA AD HAEC IVSTICIA / FORTITVDINE ANIMI CONSILIO SI NIHIL AMPLIVS. CERTE / SVMMORVM PRINCIPVM GLORIAM AEMVLARI CONTENDI. / PIETATI ERGA PATRIAM MEAE SATISFECI NVNQVAM. MAXIMA / BELLA PRO VESTRA SALVTE ET DIGNITATE TERRA MARIQVE PER / ANNOS PLVSQVAM XXX GESSI SVMMA FELICITATE CONFECI. / LABANTEM SVFFVLSI ITALIAE LIBERTATEM. TVRBATORES QVIETIS / ARMIS COMPESCVI. BRIXIAM BERGOMVM RAVENAM CREMAM / IMPERIO ADIVNXI VESTRO. OMNIBVS ORNAMENTIS PATRIAM / AVXI. PACE VOBIS PARTA ITALIA IN TRANQVILLVM FOEDERE / REDACTA POST TOT LABORES EXHAVSTOS AETATIS ANNO LXXXIIII / DVCATVS IIII SVPRA XXX SALVTISQVE MCCCCLVII KLENDIS / NOVEMBRIBVS AD AETERNAM REQVIEM COMMICRAVI. VOS / IVSTICIAM ET CONCORDIAM QVO SEMPITERNVM HOC SIT / IMPERIVM CONSERVATE." The inscription is attributed to Bernardo Giustiniani by Berlan, *op. cit.*, p. 175, and others.

5. "FRANCISCO / AVO / DIVO DVCI / FRANCISCO / GERMANO / PIENTISSIMO. // NICOLAVS / IACOBI / MONVMENTVM / HOC / MAGNIFICE / POSVIT." are inscribed on the pedestals of the left and right columns, respectively.

6. None of Doge Foscari's five sons survived him. The only son to live long enough to marry and beget children was Jacopo, who died in exile on January 12, 1457. (Berlan, *op. cit.*, p. 61.) On September 13, 1447, Jacopo already had two sons, the youngest of whom was two months old. (*Ibid.*, pp. 177f.) In a petition of September 10, 1451, Jacopo mentions four children aged seven, five, four, and two years. (Flaminio Corner, *Opuscula quatuor quibis illustrantur gesta B. Francisci Quirini, Joannis de Benedictis, Francisci Foscari, Andreae Donati*, Venice, 1758, p. 183.) From the fact that Francesco's name consistently precedes that of Niccolò in the doge's testament, we may deduce that

Francesco was the elder brother. The evidence does not suffice to permit the postulation of birth dates for Francesco and Niccolò. We can say only that at Foscari's death Francesco cannot have been more than thirteen years of age, and Niccolò not more than ten.

The doge's testament of October 29, 1457, unpublished hitherto, is interesting for what it tells us of Foscari's descendants. "In Christi nomine. Amen. Anno millesimo quatringentesimo quinquagesimo septimo, mensis Octobris, die vigesimo nono, indictione VI, Rivoalti. Testamentum magnifici domini Francisci Foscari, olim incliti ducis Venetiarum, in quo quidem instituo et esse volo meos commissarios dominum Marcum Foscari honorandum procuratorem Sancti Marci fratrem meum dilectum et Marinam peramabilem uxorem meam necnon Franciscum et Nicolaum nepotes meos, filios quondam Jacobi olim filij mej, cum pervenerint ad etatem annorum viginti. . . . Item volo et ordino quod Lucretia nurus mea stare debeat cum dicta uxore mea bene se habendo aurj tot et etiam filiis suis bene tractando eos et habeat victum et vestitum de bonis mee commissarie, quibus nepotibus meis mando ut sint obedientes ipsi matri sue sicut debent. Item dimitto ipsi Lucretie ultra id quod sibi dimitto, dilectionis amore ducatos viginti quinque aurj in anno ut de ipsi faciat quod voluerit. Residuum vero omnium bonorum meorum mobilium et immobilium presentium et futurorum, caducorum et inordinatorum dimitto suprascriptis Francisco et Nicolao nepotibus meis equaliter inter eos cum hoc conditione [quod] teneantur permanere et vivere quiete et obedientes cum ipsis uxore mea et dicta matre ipsorum, et hoc cum pervenerint ad etate viginti annorum. Ita tamen quod non possint vendere aliquam vel aliquas ex possessionibus meis nisi cum compleverint vigesimum annum. Et tunc si voluerint vendere suprascriptus dictus Marcus frater meus habeat predictas pro quindecim pro omnibus pro minori precio quo fuerit vendite in Venetiis. Cui quidem fratri meo Marco dimitto ducatos centum aurj dilectionis amore. . . ." (ASV, Archivio Notarile, Testamenti, Busta 1149 [Not. Paolo Benedetto], c. 2.)

7. See above, n. 5.

8. *Voyage de Georges Lengherand, Mayeur de Mons en Haynaut à Venise, Rome, Jérusalem, Mont Sinaï et Le Kayre, 1485–1486*, ed. Marquis de Godefroy Ménilglaise, Mons, 1861, p. 42: "Et y [at S. Maria dei Frari] a deux sépultures des ducz de Venise fort riches et sumptueuses." See also Marc'Antonio Sabellico, *Rerum Venetarum ab urbe condita ad sua usque tempora libri xxxiii*, Venice, May 21, 1487, Decade 3, Book 8, n.p. [p. 195r]. The tomb was also listed by Marin Sanudo among the "cosse notabili in diverse chiesie" compiled in 1493 and appended to his *De origine situ et magistratibus urbis Venetae (Cronachetta)*: Paoletti, 1893, ii, p. 185, n. 1.

9. Debra Dienstfrey Pincus, "A Hand by Antonio Rizzo and the Double Caritas Scheme of the Tron Tomb," *Art Bulletin*, li, 1969, p. 247, n. 1.

10. Giuseppe Merzario, *I maestri comacini*, Milan, 1893, ii, p. 25; Planiscig, *VB*, 1921, p. 32; Mariacher, *Le arti*, 1940–41, p. 194; Romanini, *Arte lombarda*, January–June 1964, pp. 91, 102, n. 4; Munman, 1968, p. xvi; Seymour, *Sculpt.*, 1966, p. 198; Hubala in Egg *et al.*, *Oberitalien Ost*, ¹1965, p. 823. A dissenting voice is that of Edoardo Arslan, "Oeuvres de jeunesse d'Antonio Rizzo," *Gazette des beaux-arts*, series 6, xlii, September 1953, p. 114, who believed that the tomb was enriched and retouched considerably after 1460. His reasons, however, are not well founded. Nor are those of Pincus, 1974, pp. 431ff., who dated the tomb to the middle or late 1480s, positing the columns, the reliefs on the sarcophagus, and the figures of the *Annunciation* as sixteenth-century additions to the tomb.

11. John Ruskin, *Stones of Venice*, London, ²1867, ii, p. 84 (iii, ch. 2, lxxi): "It [The Foscari Tomb] is remarkable chiefly as introducing all the faults of the Renaissance at an early period when its merits, such as they are, were yet undeveloped. Its claim to be rated as a classical composition is altogether destroyed by the remnants of Gothic feeling which cling to it here and there in their last forms of degradation; and of which, now that we find them thus corrupted, the sooner we are rid the better. Thus the sarcophagus is supported by a species of trefoil arches; the bases of the shafts have their spurs; and the whole tomb is covered by a pediment with crockets and a pinnacle. We shall find that the perfect Renaissance is at least pure in its insipidity, and subtle in its vice; but this monument is remarkable as showing the refuse of one style encumbering the embryo of another, and all principles of life entangled either in the swaddling clothes or the shroud."

12. For the recovery of the frescoes see Aldo Scolari, "La Chiesa di S.ta Maria Gloriosa dei Frari ed il suo recente restauro," Venice. Museo Civico Correr. *Venezia, studi di arte e storia*, i, 1920, pp. 167f.

13. Cesare Vecellio, *De gli habiti antichi, et moderni di diverse parti del mondo libri due*, Venice, 1590, pp. 77ᵛ, 79ʳ.

14. Nicolò Papadopoli, *Le monete di Venezia*, Venice, i, 1893, pp. 123ff., 137, no. 1; Herbert E. Ives, *The Vene-*

tian Gold Ducat and Its Imitations, ed. Philip Grierson (Numismatic Notes and Monographs, 128), New York, 1954, pp. 5ff.

15. In several examples of the *Ascension*, Christ, flanked by two angels, is represented in a manner identical to the *Foscari Christ*: garbed in cloak and gown, Christ stands within a *mandorla*; his right hand is raised in blessing; his left hand holds a closed book. 1) Oxford, Bodleian Library, Canon. lit. 319, *Sacramentary*, 10th to 11th century, fol. 110v. 2) Cambridge, Library of St. John's College, K. 26, *Psalter*, 13th century, fol. 21v. 3) Manchester, Rylands Library, 140, *Bible*, 13th century, fol. 243r (Christ's face, however, is covered by a cloud). 4) Rome, Pasini Collection, panel painting, second half of the 14th century. In the following example Christ is represented as above but there are no angels: Paris, Bibliothèque Nationale, N. Acq. lat. 1392, *Psalter*, Paris, first half of the 13th century, fol. 13r. In the following examples of the *Ascension* Christ is represented as above but with his right arm partially extended—in a manner, therefore, identical to the figure of Christ on the Venetian ducat. 1) Cambridge, Pembroke College Library, 16, St. Gregory, *Homiliae*, 12th century, fol. 71v (no angels). 2) Saint Gall, Stiftsbibliothek, 402, *Breviary*, first half of the 13th century, fol. 10r (two angels). In all of these examples, however, Christ is barefoot and has a halo.

For the iconography of the *Ascension* in general see E. T. Dewald, "The Iconography of the Ascension," *American Journal of Archaeology*, xix, 1915, pp. 277–319; Robert Berger, *Die Darstellung des thronenden Christus in der romanischen Kunst*, Reutlingen, 1926, pp. 173–179; Hubert Schrade, "Zur Ikonographie der Himmelfahrt Christi," *Vorträge der Bibliothek Warburg*, viii, 1928–29, pp. 66–190; S. Helena Gutberlet, *Die Himmelfahrt Christi in der bildenden Kunst*, Strasbourg, ²1935.

16. E.g., entrance wall, Badia, Pomposa.

17. For the iconography of the *Glorification of Christ* see Staale Sinding-Larsen, "Titian's Triumph of Faith and the Medieval Tradition of the Glory of Christ," *Acta ad archaeologiam et artium historiam pertinentia*, vi, 1975, pp. 315ff. esp. pp. 330f.

18. Only two Italian tombs of this period with scenes of the *Ascension* are known to me: the Tomb of the Rusconi Family, Civiche Raccolte d'Arte, Castello Sforzesco, Milan, from S. Francesco, Como, second half of the 14th century and Andrea del Verrocchio's Cenotaph of Niccolò Forteguerri, Duomo, Pistoia. In neither of these is Christ shown standing. Henriette s'Jacob, *Idealism and Realism: A Study of Sepulchral Symbolism*, Leiden, 1954, pp. 129f., cites only two

tomb slabs with scenes of the *Ascension*—one French, the other German, both of the 16th century.

19. *Ibid.*, p. 130; Erwin Panofsky, *Tomb Sculpture*, ed. H. W. Janson, London, 1964, p. 77. Ordinarily, images of the doge (as of all other men) in heaven were embodied in funerary sculpture by the scene, elevated to the tomb's lunette, of the deceased kneeling before the enthroned Madonna and Child. See Sinding-Larsen, *op. cit.*, *Acta ad archaeologiam*, 1975, pp. 324ff.

20. In addition to the Tron and Mocenigo Tombs, the scene of the *Resurrection* appears in the following tombs: Nanni di Bartolo, Tomb of Nicolò Brenzoni (d. 1422), S. Fermo Maggiore, Verona, 1426; Tomb of Doges Marco and Agostino Barbarigo (d. 1486 and 1501, respectively), formerly, S. Maria della Carità, Venice; Giovanni Dalmata and Mino da Fiesole, Tomb of the Venetian Pope Paul II (d. 1471), formerly St. Peter's, Rome, now dismembered. Although now detached from its funerary context, Michelozzo's *Resurrected Christ* in the Cathedral, Montepulciano, probably originally served the same iconographic function in the Tomb of Bartolommeo Aragazzi.

21. Dewald, *op. cit.*, *American Journal of Archaeology*, 1915, pp. 281f.

22. With its abbreviations expanded the inscription reads: "Sit tibi Christe datus, quem tu regis, iste ducatus."

23. For a discussion of the formal sources of the tomb see Meyer, *JPK*, 1889, p. 189, and s'Jacob, *Idealism and Realism*, 1954, pp. 33ff.

24. This is surely a likelier source for the unusual motif of capital surmounted by console than the Casa di Cola di Rienzo cited by Wolters, 1976, i, p. 293.

25. *Ibid.*, i, p. 293.

26. The similarity induced Fiocco, *Dedalo*, 1927–28, p. 454, to situate the Venier Tomb "nella cerchia di Antonio Bregno."

27. Sabellico, *Res Venetae*, 1487, Decade 3, Book 8, n.p. [p. 195r]: "Ex pario marmore purissimoque auro nepotes illi ad aram templi maximam posuere"; *idem*, *De Venetae urbis situ libri tres*, Venice, n.d., n.p. [p. 33r]: "ad aram maximam ducaria monumenta Francisci foscari marmore & auro praeditū." (The book was written, at least in part, in 1491: G. Mercati, *Ultimi contributi alla storia degli umanisti*, Vatican City, 1939, ii, p. 14, n. 1.)

28. An impression of the engraving is preserved at the Mus. Cor., Raccolta Gherro, ii, no. 290. The angel is

also missing in the earlier engraving of the tomb by Vincenzo Coronelli, *Singolarità di Venezia e del serenissimo suo dominio. Depositi più singolari di Venezia*, Venice, n.d. (ca. 1710) (Mus. Cor., Stampe F 10, 229), where, however, the resemblance to the Foscari Tomb is only approximate. The tomb was also engraved for Antonio Diedo and Francesco Zanotto, *I monumenti cospicui di Venezia*, Milan, 1839, n.p., inscribed below: "Querina dis.; Moretti inc." A drawing of the tomb by Antonio Battisti is preserved in the Mus. Cor., *Disegni architettura*, Inv. 155.

29. The legend to Giampiccoli's engraving reads: "Monumento del Doge Francesco Foscari esistente eretto al Lato occidentale della Capella Maggiore della Chiesa detta de' Frari in Venezia, ricoperto di dorature, e decorato di Simboleggianti Statue, mezze Figure, et l'ornamenti a basso, e tutto rilievo: opera d'invenzione dissegno, e Travaglio dell'Architetto Paulo, e dello Scultore Antonio Frattelli Bregno di Como."

The first scholar to make use of the inscription on the engraving for an attribution of the tomb was Cicognara, ii, 1816, pp. 153f., who claimed that the engraving had been made for Federigo Foscari. The attribution to the Bregno brothers, or to Antonio Bregno alone, was repeated by: Giannantonio Moschini, *Itinéraire de la ville de Venise et des îles circonvoisines*, Venice, 1819, p. 272; Burckhardt, *Cic.*, ¹1855, pp. 213d, 621f.; Meyer, *JPK*, 1889, pp. 190f.; Paoletti, 1893, i, pp. 44, ii, p. 146; Merzario, *op. cit.*, 1893, ii, p. 25; Gustav Pauli, *Venedig*, Leipzig, 1898, pp. 68f.; Paul Schubring, *Das italienische Grabmal der Frührenaissance*, Berlin, 1904, pl. xxxii. Antonio Diedo and Francesco Zanotto, *I monumenti cospicui di Venezia*, Milan, 1839, n.p. [p. 27], doubted the existence of a separate person by the name of Antonio Bregno, supposing him to be identical with Antonio Rizzo, to whom they gave the tomb. The influence of this view was soon felt, above all, in guides to Venice: Selvatico-Lazari, *Guida*, 1852, p. 178: Pietro (?) and Antonio Rizzo; Zanotto, *Nuovissima guida*, 1856, p. 464: Paolo and Antonio Rizzo; Mothes, *Geschichte*, i, 1859, p. 289: Pietro and Antonio Rizzo; Burckhardt, *Der Cicerone*, with A. von Zahn, Leipzig, ³1874, p. 670a: Antonio and Pietro (also called Paolo) Rizzo; Fulin-Molmenti, *Guida*, 1881, pp. 290f.: Pietro (?) and Antonio Rizzo; Burckhardt-Bode, *Cic.*, ⁵1884, ii, 2, p. 429a: Rizzo (or Bregno) brothers.

A more recent proponent of the attribution of the tomb to Antonio Rizzo was Venturi, *Storia*, vi, 1908, pp. 1058ff., who justified the appearance of Bregno's name in the legend of Giampiccoli's engraving by Francesco Sansovino's confusion of Rizzo and Bregno. Venturi was seconded by André Michel, *Histoire de*

l'art depuis les premiers temps chrétiens jusqu'à nos jours, Paris, iv, pt. 1, 1909, p. 192; Pierre de Bouchaud, *La sculpture vénitienne*, Paris, 1913, pp. 104f., and Venturi, *Storia*, viii, pt. 2, 1924, p. 489. However, most scholars have preferred to follow Leo Planiscig, *VB*, 1921, pp. 32ff., who, on the basis of the inscription of the engraving, reaffirmed the attribution to Antonio Bregno and assigned to the same hand the statues of *Temperance* and *Fortitude* from the Porta della Carta. He reasserted this attribution in *idem*, *VJ*, 1926, p. 95; *idem*, *VJ*, 1930, p. 101; *idem*, T-B, xxviii, 1934, p. 409. Those who expressed agreement included: Lorenzetti, ¹1926, pp. 79f., 554f.; Fiocco, *Dedalo*, 1927–28, pp. 449f.; S. Guyer, *Venice, Buildings and Sculptures* (Mirabilia Mundi, 1), trans. L. B. Ellis, Augsburg, 1928, p. xix; Géza de Francovich, "Bregno, Antonio," *Enciclopedia italiana*, Milan, vii, 1930, p. 792; Fogolari, *L'arte*, 1930, p. 458; *idem*, *I Frari e i SS. Giovanni e Paolo*, Milan, 1931, p. oppos. pl. 7; Giovanni Mariacher, "Premesse storiche alla venuta dei Lombardi a Venezia nel '400," Venice. Istituto veneto di scienze, lettere ed arti. *Atti* (Classe di scienze morali e lettere), xcvii, pt. 2, 1937–38, p. 585; *idem*, *BM*, 1950, p.124; *idem*, "Nota su due sculture veneziane al Museo Nazionale di Ravenna," *Felix Ravenna*, series 3, fasc. 6, December 1951, p. 33; A. Sartori, *Guida storico-artistica della Basilica di S. M. Gloriosa dei Frari in Venezia*, Padua, 1949, p. 105; Michelangelo Muraro, *Nuova guida di Venezia e delle sue isole*, Florence, 1953, p. 281; Pope-Hennessy, *Ital. Ren. Sc.*, ¹1958, pp. 107, 348; *idem*, *V & A Cat.*, 1964, i, p. 346; Hubala in Egg *et al.*, *Oberitalien Ost*, ¹1965, pp. 823f.; Jolán Balogh, "Studi sulla collezione di sculture del Museo di Belle Arti di Budapest. VI." *Acta historiae artium*, xii, 1966, p. 245; Seymour, *Sculpt.*, 1966, pp. 197f.; Munman, 1968, pp. xvi, 81; Pohlandt, *BJ*, 1971, p. 165; Arslan, *Ven. got.*, 1970, pp. 249, 253, n. 146; Budapest, Szépművészeti Múzeum, *Katalog der ausländischen Bildwerke des Museums der bildenden Künste in Budapest, iv.-xviii. Jahrhundert*, by Jolán Balogh, Budapest, 1975, i, p. 93, no. 105. Although Wolters, 1976, i, pp. 131f., 292f., credited the validity of Giampiccoli's attribution, the absence of any certain information concerning either of the brothers made Wolters scruple to attribute the tomb unconditionally to Antonio and Paolo Bregno. Instead, he called its author the "Maestro del Monumento Foscari."

Fiocco, *Dedalo*, 1927–28, p. 454, observed distinctions, particularly in the treatment of drapery, between the crowning figures of the tomb and those around the effigy. Mariacher, *Le arti*, 1940–41, pp. 195ff., explained those distinctions by the intervention of the young Antonio Rizzo working as Bregno's *garzone* (whose training in Bregno's shop Fiocco had already postulated). In *Arte veneta*, 1948, pp. 68, 70, Mariacher limited Rizzo's hypothetical intervention to the *Annunciate Virgin* and *Gabriel*. His attribution to Rizzo of the *Annunciation* was seconded by Arslan, *op. cit.*, *Gazette des beaux-arts*, September 1953, p. 107, and Romanini, *Arte lombarda*, January–June 1964, p. 91. Giovanni Paccagnini, "Il Mantegna e la plastica dell'Italia settentrionale," *Bollettino d'arte*, xlvi, 1961, p. 93, assigned all the crowning figures of "Bregno's" tomb to Rizzo. Hubala in Egg *et al.*, *Oberitalien Ost*, [1]1965, p. 824, thought unlikely the participation of Antonio Rizzo.

30. The project of the S. Zeno Altarpiece had already been conceived by January 5, 1457. By June 29, 1459, little work remained to be done on it, and by January 26, 1460, it had been transported from Padua to Verona. (For the dating of the altarpiece see Lionello Puppi, *Il trittico di Andrea Mantegna per la Basilica di San Zeno Maggiore in Verona*, Verona, 1972, pp. 21ff.)

31. Paoletti, "Bregno," T-B, iv, 1910, p. 568, concluded from the stylistic relationship between the Foscari Tomb and certain details of ornament and sculpture of the Arco Foscari that Antonio Bregno, and perhaps also Paolo Bregno, had participated in the construction of the Arco's upper story. (Paoletti, "Bono," T-B, iv, 1910, p. 316, noted that Bartolomeo Bon and Pantaleone di Paolo had been dismissed as architects of the Arco Foscari before the completion of its upper story.) Max Ongaro, *Il Palazzo Ducale* (Il piccolo cicerone moderno, no. 6), Milan, n.d., p. 15, n. 1, attributed to the same builders the architecture of the Foscari Tomb and the Arco Foscari. Resemblances between the two monuments were noted by: Paoletti, 1893, i, pp. 43, 78; Venturi, *Storia*, viii, pt. 2, 1924, pp. 494ff.; Fiocco, *Dedalo*, 1927–28, p. 454; Mariacher, *Pal. Duc.*, 1950, p. 22; *idem*, *BM*, 1950, p. 127; Hubala in Egg *et al.*, *Oberitalien Ost*, [1]1965, p. 824; Arslan, *Ven. got.*, 1970, p. 249; Pincus, 1974, pp. 427f.; and Wolters, 1976, i, pp. 132, 293f., who hesitantly proposed Paolo Bregno as architect of the Arco Foscari. For a thorough discussion of the attribution of the Arco Foscari see Pincus, 1974, pp. 253ff.

32. This difference in style was also noted by Wendy Stedman Sheard, *The Tomb of Doge Andrea Vendramin in Venice by Tullio Lombardo*, Ph.D. dissertation, Yale University, New Haven, Conn., 1971 (typescript), p. 463, n. 16, who explained it by a hypothetical interval of at least a decade in the construction of the fabric. Wolters, 1976, i, pp. 293f., also observed two phases of construction, although the dividing line he drew between them does not entirely

coincide with mine. Wolters, furthermore, believed that Bon was hired, not before, but after the death of the author of the Foscari Tomb (Paolo Bregno?), whose project Bon completed.

33. Giambattista Lorenzi, *Monumenti per servire alla storia del Palazzo Ducale di Venezia*, pt. 1, Venice, 1868, pp. 66ff., doc. 158.

34. Rodolfo Gallo, "Il Portico della Carta del Palazzo Ducale," *Rivista di Venezia*, xii, 1933, pp. 287, 293.

35. *Ibid.*, pp. 289ff.

36. Lorenzi, *op. cit.*, 1868, p. 584, doc. 3; Paoletti, 1893, ii, p. 153.

37. Francesco Zanotto, *Il Palazzo Ducale di Venezia*, Venice, i, 1842–53, "Storia della fabbrica," p. 79; Lorenzi, *op. cit.*, 1868, p. 83, doc. 185; Paoletti, 1893, i, pp. 40f.

38. *Res Venetae*, 1487, Decade 3, Book 9, n.p. [p. 204r]. Doubtless, this was the source of the account in Marin Sanudo, "Vite de' duchi di Venezia," in Lodovico Antonio Muratori, *Rerum Italicarum scriptores*, Milan, xxii, 1733, col. 1166, written between 1490 and 1530. Sanudo compounded Sabellico's error by describing Malipiero's arms on the Arco Foscari.

39. Paoletti, 1893, ii, p. 144.

40. Very few scholars discuss the statues individually although they vary markedly in style and quality. Paoletti, 1893, i, p. 43, noted the similarity of *St. Mark* and the *Foscari Christ*. Mariacher, *Le arti*, 1940–41, p. 194, attributed *St. Mark* to Antonio Bregno on the basis of the similarity of its drapery to that of the *Virtues* from the Foscari Tomb. Pincus, 1974, pp. 352ff., gave the figure to an anonymous Lombard sculptor and dated it to the early 1480s.

41. Paoletti, 1893, i, p. 43, was the first to note the similarity of its style to that of the Foscari Tomb. The *Gorgon Warrior* was related to the right-hand *Foscari Page* by Venturi, *Storia*, vi, 1908, p. 1068 (who therefore attributed it to Rizzo); Fogolari, *Pal. Duc.*, p. oppos. pl. 9 (who therefore assigned it to a Tuscan follower of Ghiberti); Mariacher, *Le arti*, 1940–41, p. 194; *idem*, *Arte veneta*, 1948, pp. 68f.; *idem*, *BM*, 1950, p. 127 (who therefore attributed it to Antonio Bregno). Pincus, 1974, pp. 328, 334ff., dated this figure to the 17th century.

42. Paoletti, i, pp. 43f., found this figure different in style from the *Gorgon Warrior* and from the figures of the Foscari Tomb. Diverse attributions were proposed by: Allan Marquand, "Two Works of Venetian Sculpture," *Art in America*, vi, 1917–18, pp. 59f.:

Antonio Rizzo; Planiscig, *VB*, 1921, p. 169: Giovanni Minelli under the influence of Mantegna; Fogolari, *Pal. Duc.*, p. oppos. pl. 9: Rizzo; Mariacher, *Le arti*, 1940–41, p. 194; idem, *Arte veneta*, 1948, pp. 68f.: Antonio Bregno. Mariacher perceived no distinction in style or quality—which he did not think very high— between the two *Warriors*. Pohlandt, *BJ*, 1971, p. 179, posited the influence of the so-called *Mars* attributed to Antonio Rizzo on the *Moro Warrior*. Indeed, the similarities are evident, but the influence is more likely to have operated in the opposite direction. Pincus, 1974, pp. 342ff., attributed this figure to the "Master of the Giustiniani Tomb" who, she believed, was also responsible for the Monument to Federico Cornaro in the Cappella Cornaro, S. Maria dei Frari, assigned by Sansovino to an otherwise unknown "Jacomo Padovano."

43. For the meaning of this image on the obverse of the Venetian ducat see Staale Sinding-Larsen, "Christ in the Council Hall. Studies in the Religious Iconography of the Venetian Republic," with a contribution by A. Kuhn, *Acta ad archaeologiam et artium historiam pertinentia*, v, 1974, pp. 159ff.

44. *Music* was linked with the Foscari Tomb by Paoletti, 1893, i, p. 43; Venturi, *Storia*, vi, 1908, p. 1068 (who therefore attributed it to Rizzo); Fogolari, *Pal. Duc.*, p. oppos. pl. 9 (who therefore attributed it to a Tuscan follower of Ghiberti). Mariacher, *Le arti*, 1940–41, pp. 197f., noting resemblances to the *Annunciate Virgin* from the portal of the Madonna dell'Orto, assigned *Music* to Antonio Rizzo. In *Arte veneta*, 1948, p. 69, Mariacher remarked the superior quality of *Music* and its reflection of the Bregnesque schemata of the *Foscari Virtues* but did not assign the figure any author. Elena Bassi and Egle Renata Trincanato, *Il Palazzo Ducale nella storia e nell'arte di Venezia*, Milan, 1960, p. 46, attributed the figure to Antonio Bregno. Pohlandt, *BJ*, 1971, p. 204, considered *Music* a derivative of the *Virtues* of the Porta della Carta. Pincus, 1974, pp. 352ff., attributed *Music* to an anonymous Lombard sculptor working in the early 1480s (not, however, the author of *St. Mark* or *Rhetoric*).

45. *Rhetoric* was linked with the Foscari Tomb by Paoletti, 1893, i, p. 43, and Fogolari, *Pal. Duc.*, p. oppos. pl. 9 (for whom its author, therefore, was a Tuscan follower of Ghiberti). Mariacher, *Le arti*, 1940–41, fig. 7, assigned the figure to Antonio Bregno and his shop. In *idem*, *Arte veneta*, 1948, pp. 70f., figs. 82, 83, *Rhetoric* was labeled "Antonio Rizzo (?)." Bassi and Trincanato, *op. cit.*, 1960, p. 46, gave *Rhetoric* to Antonio Bregno. Romanini, *Arte lombarda*, January– June 1964, p. 93, fig. 5, gave it to Antonio Rizzo.

Pincus, 1974, pp. 352ff., attributed *Rhetoric* to a third anonymous Lombard sculptor working in the early 1480s.

46. *Mon. Ven.*, ii, 1754, p. 50.

47. Antonio Santalena, *Leoni di S. Marco*, Venice, 1906, pp. 7ff.

48. For the meaning of the image see Sinding-Larsen, *op. cit.*, *Acta ad archaeologiam*, 1974, p. 165.

49. Hans Conrad Peyer, "Venedig und Marcus," *Stadt und Stadtpatron im mittelalterlichen Italien*, Zurich, 1955, pp. 18f.

50. Selvatico-Lazari, *Guida*, 1852, p. 54, considered the group "opera della scuola lombardesca." The group was attributed with a greater or lesser degree of confidence to Antonio Rizzo by Zanotto, *Nuovissima guida*, 1856, p. 124, n. 2; Charles Perkins, *Historical Handbook of Italian Sculpture*, New York, 1883, p. 212, n. ‡; Paoletti, "Bregno," T-B, iv, 1910, p. 568; Antonio della Rovere, *Il Palazzo Ducale in Venezia*, Mestre, n.d., pp. 7f. Mariacher, *BM*, 1950, p. 127, n. 6, attributed the group to Antonio Bregno. Pincus, 1974, pp. 373ff., identified a ducal portrait displayed in the second-story loggia of the Ducal Palace as a fragment of the kneeling figure of *Moro* from the Arco Foscari and claimed it as an early work, dated ca. 1464, by Antonio Rizzo. But a comparison with authentic portraits of the doge reveals that this bust does not represent Moro. Particularly at variance with the physiognomy of Moro is its receding chin. Nor is there any reason for attributing this inferior work to Antonio Rizzo, with whose portrait of Niccolò Tron it has nothing in common.

51. Bibl. Marc., Cod. it., Cl. VII, 791 (=7589), *Cronaca Veniera* (containing events up to 1580), fol. 151v: "1464. A di 4 Auosto el fu fatto l'essequio de messer Orsato Justiniani Cavalier et Procurator et Capitano Zeneral da mar, el qual morj in Armada come ho ditto di sopra el corpo fu condutto con la sua gallia in una cassa, et fu mandato per li suoi a Santo Andrea de Lido della Certosa, & sepelido in una rica Capella in una Archa de Marmoro in meza la ditta Capella come al presente si vede, et questo fu quando fu portato il suo Corpo, et li fu fatto uno novelissimo essequio cominciando da S. Marco fino a S. Zuane Polo, & forno tutti frati de S. Domenigo, et de S. Francesco: & la scolla di battudi, et la Signoria con piu de 200 Zentillhomini et tutti li Ambascatorj che' se' trouauano esser a' Venetia, et forno tutta la chieresia, et cauallj 20 coverti de pani negri con alcuni homini a cavallo vestiti de corotto comperti la testa con i capuzi, et non se li vedeva pur la fazza, li quali havevano in

mano certe Bandiere negre, le quale andavano stras-sinado per terra, et fu fatto uno dignissimo sermone in laude sua & della sua casada." Marin Sanudo, *Sommary di storia Venetiana*, as quoted by Cicogna, *Delle inscrizioni*, iv, 1834, p. 629, gives the date of Giustiniani's funeral as August 3 and tells us that the funeral oration was delivered by Caldiera.

52. Giustiniani's testament, unpublished hitherto, was notarized by Benedetto de Soris da Venezia. ASV, Procuratori di S. Marco de citra, Filza 117, Busta O, II, no. 2, c. 13r: "Apresso voio pur de i soraditi danari he a la procolatia a zan da brazo chastoldo a la dita ducati 300 zioe ducati trexento per far conpir a Santo Andrea da la Certoxa la mia seputura e sel mancase niente Marin suplisa a quella perche lui fa come lui la die far." *Ibid.*, c. 14r: "Io fina sara fata la mia archa. voio essere messo in una cassa e atorno un monu-mento de tole [tavole] cum le mie Arme segondo usanza. e se zan da brazo non fosse vivo larcha per i procolatori sia fata far per la qual io ordeno ducati 300."

53. Orsato had only two illegitimate daughters of his own. See Cicogna, *Delle inscrizioni*, ii, 1827, p. 57.

54. ASV, Procuratori di S. Marco de citra, Filza 117, Busta O, II, no. 2, c. 24r:

"Dabimus ser Johannes de Brazo ducatos trecentos auri pro faciendo sepulcrum nostri comissi iuxta testamentum suum iuxta etiam sententiam latam ad comissariam pro cetero in puncto testamenti M CCCC LXVI die XXII aprilis dedimus suprascripto ser Johanni pro parte dictorum ducatorum trecento-rum portavit ipse
lire di grossi XX   soldi – denari –
"Eodem die dedimus notario cancellerie procurato-rum pro sua mercede suprascripte sententie portavit ipse per Andree Ingegnerio plebano S. Thome notario
lire di grossi   soldi II denari VI
"Eodem millesimo die primo mensis dezembris dedi-mus suprascripto ser Johanni pro resto ducatorum trecentorum pro faciendo sepulcrum suum iuxta testamentum suum portavit ipse ducatos centum auri
lire di grossi 10   soldi – denari –"

55. "ILLE PROCVRATOR VENETA / MODO MAXIMVS VRBE / ORSATVS IACET HIC IVSTI / NIANVS EQVES. / QVI TVRCOS BIMARI CLASSIS / PRAEFECTVS AB ISTHMO / DVM FVGAT O FATVM QVAN / TA TROPHEA RAPIS / DECESSIT ANN. X. MCCCCLX / IIII. V. IDVS QVINT. / MARINVS IVSTINI / ANVS PATRVO / DE SE BENEME / RITO EXTRVI / CVRAVIT." For the inscription see Cicogna, *Delle inscrizioni*, ii, 1827, pp. 55, 58.

56. The chapel and tomb are described by the *Cronaca Veniera*, fol. 151v, quoted above, n. 35, and by Sanudo, *Sommary di storia Venetiana*, quoted by Cicogna, *Delle inscrizioni*, iv, 1834, p. 629: "l corpo sepulto poi ala Zertosa in una capella fata dil suo in una bellissima archa marmorea alta in mezo di deta capella." The Giustiniani Tomb occurs in the list of "cosse notabili in diverse chiesie" compiled by Marin Sanudo in 1493: Paoletti, 1893, ii, p. 185, n. 1. It is also mentioned by Sabellico, *De Venetae urbis situ libri tres*, [1491], n.p. [p. 51r]: "uisit hic ursati iustiniani ex pario marmore sepulchrum affabre caelatum."

57. Vincenzo Coronelli, *Isolario dell'atlante veneto*, Ven-ice, 1696, i, p. 45; Cicogna, *Delle inscrizioni*, ii, 1827, pp. 51, 57.

58. *Ibid.*, p. 52; John McAndrew, "Sant'Andrea della Certosa," *Art Bulletin*, li, 1969, p. 18.

59. *Mon. Ven.*, i, 1754, p. 92.

60. Vecellio, *Habiti antichi*, 1590, pp. 83rf.

61. Robert Munman, "Antonio Rizzo's Sarcophagus for Nicolò Tron: A Closer Look," *Art Bulletin*, lv, 1973, p. 81, n. 6.

62. Munman, 1968, pp. 63f.

63. Inv. no. E I-18. The life-size standing figure is wrapped in a himation worn over a chiton. Carved from Greek marble, it is missing its head. The statue is dated to the 1st century A.D. (Giulio Fasolo, *Guida del Museo Civico di Vicenza*, Vicenza, 1948, p. 10, no. 18.) The figure was traditionally said to have come from the Roman Teatro Berga at Vicenza of which very little remained standing by the 15th century. (*Ibid.*, p. 11; Bernardo Morsolin, "L'acquedotto romano e il Teatro Berga di Vicenza," Venice. R. Deputazione veneta di storia patria. *Miscellanea*, iii, 1885 [1884], p. 14.) It is therefore very likely that the statue was known during the Middle Ages and early Renaissance. Seventeenth- and 18th-century guides to Vicenza situate the statue in the chapel of S. Giovanni Battista in the fifth bay from the entrance in the left aisle of the Vicentine church of S. Corona. The statue stood on a base against the west face of the northwest crossing pier. Beneath the statue was the following inscription: "IPHIGENIA POST VESTALES PRIMA VIRGO DEO DICATA." Facing the an-tique draped figure, standing against the east face of the next pier to the west, was a second antique figure which had been stolen by the early 17th century. (The position of our statue is most amply described in a manuscript of ca. 1628 by Silvestro Castellini entitled *Descrizione della città e borghi di Vicenza*, quoted by Domenico Bortolan, *S. Corona, chiesa e convento dei*

domenicani in Vicenza, Vicenza, 1889, pp. 267f. See also Francesco Barbarano, *Historia ecclesiastica della città, territorio e diocese di Vicenza*, Vicenza, v, 1761, p. 166; [Pietro Baldarini, Enea Arnaldi, Orzio Vecchia, Lodovico Buffetti], *Descrizione delle architetture, pitture e scolture di Vicenza, con alcune osservazioni*, Vicenza, 1779, pt. 1, pp. 14f.; Silvestro Castellini, *Descrizione della città di Vicenza dentro dalle mura*, ed. D. Bortolan, Vicenza, 1885, p. 85.) The chapel of which the statue was a part was appropriated to Giambattista Graziano Garzadori on November 2, 1500. In that same year, we learn from an inscription, the chapel was dedicated in fulfilment of a vow which Garzadori had made in Palestine. (The inscription is divided between the north faces of the two piers against which the antique statues were placed. It reads: "GRATIANVS / HIEROSOLYMIS / SOSPES / HOC SACELLVM / DIVO IOANNI / DICAVIT / / ANNO / MD." For the history of the chapel see Bortolan, *S. Corona*, 1889, pp. 267ff.) Construction of the chapel began in 1501. Its chief ornament was the colossal painting by Giovanni Bellini of the *Baptism of Christ* which is still there today. The early 17th-century description of Vicenza referred to above states that our antique female figure was installed against the crossing pier by Garzadori himself. (Castellini, *Descrizione*, quoted by Bortolan, *S. Corona*, 1889, p. 267; Castellini, *Descrizione*, 1885, p. 85.) Our statue is probably the "bellissima statua antica in Santa Corona" whose fine-grained white marble elicited lengthy comment from Vincenzo Scamozzi, *L'idea della architettura universale*, Venice, 1615, Pt. II, Bk. 7, ch. v, p. 189. The statue was transferred from S. Corona to the Museo Civico at Vicenza in 1856. (Bortolan, *S. Corona*, 1889, p. 268.)

64. I.e., *Charity*, main portal of the Scuola di S. Marco; *Charity*, Porta della Carta, Ducal Palace; *Arithmetic*, Arco Foscari. See Anne Markham Schulz, "The Sculpture of Giovanni and Bartolomeo Bon and Their Workshop," *Transactions of the American Philosophical Society*, in press. This antique prototype also inspired: *Madonna and Child* over the main entrance of S. Michele in Isola; female figure on extreme right in Antonio Lombardo's *Miracle of the Speaking Babe*, 1505, Cappella del Santo, S. Antonio, Padua; left female figure in Tullio Lombardo's *Tomb of Giovanni Mocenigo*, 1522, SS. Giovanni e Paolo.

65. *VJ*, 1926, pp. 94f. Actually, however, Planiscig was not the first to connect the three *Virtues* with the Giustiniani Tomb. *Temperance* had been acquired by Count Gregory Stroganoff in Venice with a provenance from the Giustiniani Tomb. (Antonio Muñoz

in Ludwig Pollak and Muñoz, *Pièces de choix de la collection du Comte Grégoire Stroganoff. II. Moyenâge, renaissance, époque moderne*, Rome, 1911, p. 117.) In 1924, *Temperance*, which in the meantime had passed into the collection of Camillo Castiglione, Vienna, and *Hope* and *Charity*, in the collection of Bruno Kern, Vienna, were all exhibited as coming from the Giustiniani Tomb. (Vienna. Secession. Vereins der Museumsfreunde in Wien, *Meisterwerke italienischer Renaissancekunst aus Privatbesitz*, 1924, exhibition catalogue, p. 14, nos. 89–91. See also Amsterdam, Frederik Muller et Cie., November 17–20, 1925, *Collections Camillo Castiglioni de Vienne, .I. Catalogue des tableaux, sculptures, meubles etc.*, p. 32, no. 110, where reference was made to Grevembroch's drawing of the Giustiniani Tomb published by Paoletti, 1893, ii, p. 144, fig. 11.)

For the provenance of the two figures in the Kress Collection, see Ulrich Middeldorf, *Sculptures from the Samuel H. Kress Collection. European Schools, XIV–XIX Century*, London, 1976, p. 63. *Hope* was purchased from the Blumka Gallery by the Metropolitan Museum in 1956. ("Additions to the Collections," New York. Metropolitan Museum of Art. *Bulletin*, n.s., xv, no. 2, October 1956, p. 46; John Goldsmith Phillips, "Recent Accessions of European Sculpture," New York. Metropolitan Museum of Art. *Bulletin*, n.s., xv, no. 6, February 1957, p. 150; letter of June 13, 1975, from Johanna Hecht, Department of Western European Arts, Metropolitan Museum of Art.)

66. Giovanni Mariacher, "Due inedite sculture di Antonio Rizzo," *Rivista d'arte*, xxvii, 1951–52, pp. 187ff. The successful identifications of the Giustiniani figures were preceded by an earlier attempt. In 1827 Cicogna, *Delle inscrizioni*, ii, p. 57, had written that the figure of *Faith* from the Giustiniani Tomb had been saved and was then in the possession of Don Bruno Stiore, abbot of S. Pietro di Castello and former Carthusian monk. Subsequently, the figure described by Cicogna was identified with a figure found in the storeroom of the Museo Archeologico in the Palazzo Ducale and exhibited for some time in the museum of the Doge's Palace in the Camera degli Stucchi. It later passed to the Galleria dell'Accademia, but for the past several decades has been displayed at the Ca' d'Oro where, called "Figura allegorica," "Rhetorica," or "Fede," it is attributed to Antonio Rizzo. (The statuette's provenance was first designated as the Giustiniani Tomb by Selvatico-Lazari, *Guida*, 1852, p. 210. This misinformation was repeated until 1926.) Even before his article of 1926, however, Planiscig, *VB*, 1921, p. 63, had expressed doubts regarding the identi-

fication which Venturi, *Storia*, vi, 1908, pp. 1060f., n. 2, had rejected outright. For the statuette in the Ca' d'Oro, see also Fogolari, Nebbia, Moschini, *La R. Galleria Giorgio Franchetti alla Ca' d'Oro, Guida-Catalogo*, Venice, 1929, pp. 79f., and Venice. Procuratie Nuove. *Arte a Venezia dal medioevo al settecento*, 1971, exhibition catalogue by Giovanni Mariacher, Venice, 1971, p. 142, no. 67, with bibliography.

67. 1581, p. 80r: "Et è [Orsato Giustiniani] riposto sopra vn cassone di marmo nel mezzo d'vna cappella, con la statua a giacere, scolpita da Antonio Dentone per ordine di Marino Giustiniani, . . ." This provided Grevembroch, *Mon. Ven.*, i, 1754, p. 92, with some of the information incorporated into the caption of his drawing: "Mausoleo scolpito da Antonio Dentone nel marmo da Carrara, e collocato nella vecchia Chiesa nell'Isola della Certosa, il tutto dedicato dal Pronipote Marino al prestantissimo Zio Orsato K.r [Cavaliere] P.r [Procuratore] di gran nome in Italia, che morì a Modone, come attesta il Sabellico, ed altri gravi Autori, la di cui Epigrafe registrammo nel seguente Foglio ad onore della Famiglia de' Giustiniani."

68. The attribution to Dentone was adopted by: Cicognara, ii, 1816, p. 174; Cicogna, *Delle inscrizioni*, ii, 1827, p. 57; Stefano Ticozzi, *Dizionario degli architetti, scultori, pittori*, Milan, i, 1830, p. 406; Giannantonio Moschini, *La chiesa e il seminario di S.ta Maria della Salute in Venezia*, Venice, 1842, p. 46; Selvatico, *Sulla architettura*, 1847, p. 228; Mothes, *Geschichte*, ii, 1860, p. 156; Fulin-Molmenti, *Guida*, 1881, pp. 340, 435; Meyer, *JPK*, 1889, p. 194.

69. *Ibid.*, p. 194.

70. Paoletti, 1893, ii, pp. 144, 226.

71. For the "Allegorical Figure" see above, n. 66. Paoletti's attribution of the Giustiniani Tomb to Antonio Rizzo was welcomed by Burckhardt-Bode-Fabriczy, *Cic.*, 7 1898, ii, 1, p. 122c, 122d; Venturi, *Storia*, vi, 1908, pp. 1060f.; Michel, *Histoire de l'art*, iv, pt. 1, 1909, pp. 193f.; Muñoz, *Collection . . . Stroganoff*, ii, 1911, p. 117.

72. Planiscig, *VJ*, 1926, pp. 96f., who, however, observed the inferior quality of the three figures he published. The attribution to Rizzo was repeated by: New York. A. S. Drey Galleries. *Sculpture of the Italian Renaissance*, March 1935, exhibition catalogue, p. 14, no. 33; Brooklyn, N.Y., Institute of Arts and Sciences. Museum. *European Art 1450-1500 presented by the Rockefeller Foundation Internes of the Brooklyn Museum*, 1936, exhibition catalogue, no. 52; Giuseppe Fiocco, "Rizzo, Antonio," *Enciclopedia italiana*, Milan, xxix, 1936, p. 502; Detroit. Institute of

Arts. *Italian Gothic and Early Renaissance Sculptures*, 1938, exhibition catalogue by W. R. Valentiner, nos. 93, 94; Carlo Ragghianti, "La mostra di scultura italiana antica a Detroit (U.S.A.)," *Critica d'arte*, iii, 1938, p. 183; Ulrich Middeldorf, "Die Ausstellung italienischer Renaissanceskulptur in Detroit," *Pantheon*, xxii, 1938, p. 318, and Mariacher, *Arte veneta*, 1948, pp. 69f., who, in addition to similarities between *Hope* and *Charity* and the worshiping *Angels* of the Arco Foscari not visible to me, noted the resemblance of *Temperance* to "le Allegorie dell'Arco verso il cortile." He further observed a link between the Giustiniani figures and the Foscari Tomb. Mariacher, *BM*, 1950, p. 127, esp. n. 10, emphasized the "striking resemblance" of *Hope*, *Charity*, and *Temperance* to the *Virtues* of the Foscari Tomb and the *Angels* of the Arco Foscari. Nevertheless, he gave the Giustiniani Tomb to the young Rizzo, albeit with the collaboration and under the influence of Bregno. Mariacher has persisted in attributing the tomb to Rizzo, though he sometimes qualifies this attribution by the postulation of Bregno's influence: Mariacher, *Rivista d'arte*, 1951-52, pp. 187f.; idem, *Antonio Rizzo* (I maestri della scultura, no. 35), Milan, 1966, n.p. [p. 3f.]; Venice. Procuratie Nuove. *Arte a Venezia dal medioevo al settecento*, 1971, exhibition catalogue by Mariacher, Venice, 1971, p. 139.

Recent studies reiterate the attribution of the tomb to Rizzo or his shop: Pope-Hennessy, *Ital. Ren. Sc.*, 1 1958, pp. 107, 349; El Paso, Texas. Museum of Art. *The Samuel H. Kress Collection*, catalogue by Fern Rusk Shapley, El Paso, 1961, no. 21; Romanini, *Arte lombarda*, January-June 1964, pp. 92f.; Munman, 1968, pp. 102f.; Pincus, *op. cit.*, Art Bulletin, 1969, p. 251; Munman, *BM*, 1971, pp. 138f. McAndrew, *op. cit.*, Art Bulletin, 1969, pp. 24f., esp. n. 44, resurrected the name of Antonio Dentone whom he credited with Giustiniani's effigy. Rizzo too, he thought, might have worked on the tomb. After an extensive examination of Rizzo's works, Pohlandt, *BJ*, 1971, p. 200, found the attribution of the Giustiniani Tomb to Rizzo unsubstantiated. The solution to the dilemma of its authorship which she cautiously advanced was its attribution to the elusive and problematical Antonio Dentone. Middeldorf, *Sculptures from the Samuel H. Kress Collection*, p. 63, could not adjudicate between the claims of Rizzo, Bregno, and Dentone. Pincus, 1974, pp. 346ff., attributed the Giustiniani Tomb to a close associate of Rizzo responsible also for the Monument to Federico Cornaro in the Cappella Cornaro, S. Maria dei Frari, and the *Moro Warrior* from the Arco Foscari. She believed, however, that only *Hope* was autograph—the other figures having been executed by an assistant. *Ibid.*, p. 351, Pincus dated the tomb to the 1480s, probably after 1485. The reason given for this late dating was the derivation of the Giustiniani sarcophagus from the Tomb of Niccolò Tron!

73. The pose and gesture of the lowered arm and hand of *Charity* recur later in the figure of *Prudence* from the Tron Tomb. This analogy, probably accountable by a common source, would support an attribution to Rizzo of the Giustiniani figure were it not for the absolute diversity of the pose, proportions, and drapery of the two figures.

74. "D · IM / VICTOR CAPPELLVS IMPERATOR MARITI / MVS MAXIMIS REBVS GESTIS III ET LX / ANNOS NATVS AB ANNO SALVTIS M̊CCCCLXVII / III IDVS MARCIAS IN EVBOIA PERRIT HIS EIVS / OSSA IN CAELO ANIMA." See also Cicogna, *Delle inscrizioni*, iii, 1830, p. 375.

75. Laura Giannasi, "Cappello, Vettore," *Dizionario biografico degli italiani*, Rome, xviii, 1975, p. 826.

76. Marin Sanudo, "Vite de' duchi di Venezia," in Lodovico Antonio Muratori, *Rerum Italicarum scriptores*, Milan, xxii, 1733, col. 1184: "Il suo corpo fu portato in questa Terra, e fattegli solenni esequie fu messo in un deposito nella Chiesa di Santa Elena."

77. Bibl. Marc., Cod. it., Cl. VII, 1676 (=9037), *Cose spettanti al Monastero di S. Elena*, fol. 121; "La sepultura poscia Capelli e imediamente unita al didentro alla soglia della porta in terra con l'arma di detto casato in mezzo, quale parimente vedesi in prospetto ne specchi de piedistalli, e al disopra di qua, . . ." Indeed, the epitaph quoted above, n. 74, says explicitly that Capello's "bones lie here."

78. "ANDREAS LODOVICVS / PAVLVS FILII PIENTISSIMI // PARENTI OPTVMO / POSVERVNT." Besides three sons, Capello had six daughters. See Cicogna, *Delle inscrizioni*, iii, 1830, p. 375.

79. The date of the tomb is not documented: a dating shortly after Capello's death is generally accepted but cannot be proven. Arguments for a later dating of ca. 1476 based on the architecture of the tomb propounded by Mariacher, *Arte veneta*, 1948, pp. 72f., were effectively refuted by Romanini, *Arte lombarda*, January–June 1964, pp. 92f. A dating in the 1470s or early 1480s posited by Pincus, *op. cit.*, *Art Bulletin*, 1969, p. 251, n. 21, was retracted in her later dissertation: Pincus, 1974, p. 173, n. 3, p. 310, n. 106.

80. The church of S. Elena was suppressed in 1807. (Rodolfo Gallo, "La Chiesa di Sant'Elena," *Rivista di Venezia*, v, 1926, pp. 480f.) Thanks to the bishop of Udine, Emanuele Lodi, then parish priest of SS. Giovanni e Paolo, the statuary and sarcophagus were reinstalled on the lateral wall just outside the entrance to the Cappella del Rosario in the left transept of SS. Giovanni e Paolo. (Cicogna, *Delle inscrizioni*, iii, 1830, p. 375; A. Sagredo, "Note sugli ammiglioramenti di Venezia," *Annali universali di statistica* [Milan], lxxvii, July-September 1843, p. 197.) They were first recorded there in 1819. (Giannantonio Moschini, *Itinéraire de la ville de Venise et des îles circonvoisines*, Venice, 1819, p. 42. Cicognara, ii, 1816, p. 174, had recorded them still *in situ* at S. Elena.) The reinstallation of the architectural portions of the tomb, which up till then had remained at S. Elena, around the exterior of the main portal of S. Aponal, took place in October 1841 preparatory to the reopening of the church. (Cicogna, *Delle inscrizioni*, iii, 1830, p. 375; Moschini, *La chiesa . . . della Salute*, 1842, p. 55, n. 1; Gallo, *op. cit.*, *Rivista di Venezia*, 1926, pp. 485, 520, doc. xli.) The vase crowning the lunette was preserved over the altar of the oratory of the Seminario Patriarcale at S. Maria della Salute where it was recorded by Moschini. (Moschini, *La chiesa . . . della Salute*, 1842, p. 55. A footnote to Moschini's posthumous book stated that the vase had recently been consigned to S. Aponal: *ibid.*, p. 55, n. 1. But it was explicitly described at the Seminario Patriarcale in 1860 by Mothes, *Geschichte*, ii, 1860, p. 156.) Certainly by 1893 the vase had been reunited with the architecture of the tomb on the facade of S. Aponal. (Paoletti, 1893, ii, p. 145, fig. 14.) In 1901 the statuary and sarcophagus were reinstalled within the architecture of the tomb. (Franca Zava Boccazzi, *La Basilica dei Santi Giovanni e Paolo in Venezia*, Padua, 1965, p. 342, n. 77; Pietro Paoletti, "Notizie di Venezia," *L'arte*, v, 1902, p. 125; cf. Gallo, *op. cit.*, *Rivista di Venezia*, 1926, p. 485. A previous attempt had been made to reintegrate the statuary with the portal in 1878: Bibl. Marc., Cod. it., Cl. VII, 2283 [= 9121], Francesco Fapanni, *Chiese claustrali e monasteri di Venezia*, fol. 70v.)

81. Munman, *BM*, 1971, p. 141.

82. In his drawing of the tomb, Grevembroch, *Mon. Ven.*, iii, 1759, p. 41, depicts a metal crown.

83. Munman, *BM*, 1971, p. 141, noted that *St. Helen*'s hand was still in place when the statues were exhibited in SS. Giovanni e Paolo.

84. S. Pozzi, "Un portrait du Général Vittore Cappello, plaquette inédite d'Ant. Rizzo," *Revue numismatique*, series 4, xviii, 1914, p. 303, n. 1.

85. Munman, *BM*, 1971, p. 142.

86. This iconographic connection was first made by Meyer, *JPK*, 1889, p. 194. For examples of this image on the Venetian ducat see Papadopoli, *Le monete di Venezia*, i, 1893, pls. viii, nos. 2, 8; ix, nos. 3, 5, 11; x,

nos. 3, 7; xi, nos. 1, 5, 11; xii, nos. 1, 5, 9; xiii, nos. 1, 5, 12; xiv, no. 5; xv, no. 1; xvi, nos. 1, 6. The earliest example is a gold ducat from the principate of Giovanni Dandolo (1280–89).

87. Leopoldo Cicognara, Giannantonio Selva, Antonio Diedo, *Le fabbriche più cospicue di Venezia*, Venice, ii, [1]1820, p. 155 ("A. Mezzani mis. e dis., Dala inc."); Antonio Quadri, *I due templi de' SS. Giovanni e Paolo e di Santa Maria Gloriosa detta de' Frari in Venezia*, Venice, 1835, pl. xiv, no. 23; Paoletti, *Il fiore*, ii, 1839, pl. oppos. p. 240; Diedo and Zanotto, *I monumenti cospicui*, 1839, n.p. ("Querena dis., Musitelli inc."). See also Munman, *BM*, 1971, p. 142.

88. The engraving illustrated in Cicognara, ii, 1816, pl. xxxix, presumably made before the statues were transferred, shows something thicker than a baton, truncated at the top just above the saint's hand and rounded at the bottom.

89. Grevembroch, *Mon. Ven.*, iii, 1759, p. 41, shows a Latin cross held by both *Capello* and *St. Helen*, which rests on the common base of the two statues and rises nearly to the top of the interior of the lunette.

90. Bibl. Marc., Cod. it., Cl. VII, 1676 (= 9037), fol. 120: "Regge essa [St. Helen] nella manca parte la croce."

91. Munman, *BM*, 1971, p. 142.

92. Sansovino, 1581, p. 78r: "Percioche ui [in the church of S. Elena] giacciono, cominciandosi dalla porta principale molto ornata, Vittorio Cappello, la cui statua pedestre fatta di finissimo marmo pario al naturaie [*sic*] da Antonio Dentone Scultor Vinitiano & di gran nome al suo tempo, è posta inginocchioni dinanzi a Santa Helena." Earlier mentions of the tomb contain no reference to its author: Sanudo "Vite de' duchi" in Muratori, *Rerum Italicarum scriptores*, xxii, 1733, col. 1184, and *idem*, *De origine situ et magistratibus urbis Venetae (Cronachetta)*, 1493, quoted by Paoletti, 1893, ii, p. 185, n. 1. Nor does that of Pietro Gradenigo, "Notizie d'arte tratte dai notatori e dagli annali del N. H. Pietro Gradenigo," ed. Lina Livan, Reale Deputazione di storia patria per le Venezie. *Miscellanea di studi e memorie*, v, Venice, 1942, p. 133. Sansovino's attribution, on the other hand, was adopted by Grevembroch, *Mon. Ven.*, iii, 1759, p. 41; Cicognara, ii, 1816, p. 174; Moschini, *Itinéraire de la ville de Venise*, 1819, p. 42; Diedo in Cicognara, Selva, Diedo, *Le fabbriche più cospicue di Venezia*, Venice, ii, [1]1820, p. 154, and Cicognara in *ibid.*, pp. 74rf.; Giambattista Soràvia, *Le chiese di Venezia descritte ed illustrate*, Venice, i, 1822, p. 105; Cicogna, *Delle inscrizioni*, iii, 1830, p. 375; Ticozzi, *Dizionario*, i, 1830, p. 406; Quadri, *I due templi*, 1835,

p. xviii, no. 23; Paoletti, *Il fiore*, i, 1837, pp. 200f.; Zanotto in Diedo and Zanotto, *I monumenti cospicui*, 1839, n.p.; A. Sagredo, "Architettura, scultura e calcografia," in *Venezia e le sue lagune*, Venice, 1847, i, pt. 2, p. 407; Selvatico, *Sulla architettura*, 1847, pp. 228f.; Selvatico-Lazari, *Guida*, 1852, pp. 124, 169; Burckhardt, *Cic.*, [1]1855, p. 628b; Zanotto, *Nuovissima guida*, 1856, pp. 294, 380; Mothes, *Geschichte*, ii, 1860, p. 156; Fulin-Molmenti, *Guida*, 1881, pp. 226, 278, 292f., 436; Camillo Boito, *Gite di un artista*, Milan, 1884, p. 73; Meyer, *JPK*, 1889, p. 194.

93. Paoletti, 1893, ii, pp. 142, 145. Without rejecting the postulation of a relationship with works of Rizzo's, Paoletti, "Bregno," *T-B*, iv, 1910, p. 569, in a shift of emphasis, stressed the likeness of *St. Helen* to the *Virtues* of the Foscari Tomb, which to him was so compelling that he ventured to hypothesize the identity of Bregno and Dentone.

94. Venturi, *Storia*, vi, 1908, p. 1061, proposed that Rizzo had delegated the execution of *St. Helen* to an assistant "riconoscibile nel drappo bagnato e strizzato." With this assistant he cautiously identified the author of the figures of the *Annunciation* of the Foscari Tomb, the statues of the portal of the Madonna dell' Orto and, strangely, the figures crowning the lunette of the portal of the Scuola di S. Marco. Venturi, *ibid.*, p. 1064, hesitantly gave this assistant the name of Giorgio da Carona, a stonemason employed by Rizzo in the construction of the Ducal Palace. Venturi's analysis was faithfully repeated by Bouchaud, *La sculpture vénitienne*, 1913, p. 110. Munman, *BM*, 1971, pp. 141f., attributed *Capello* and *St. Helen*, the latter of which he believed to be the poorer of the figures, to two anonymous sculptors. See also an earlier version of this argument in Munman, 1968, pp. 68ff., 103.

95. Pozzi, *op. cit.*, *Revue numismatique*, 1914, p. 206; Paul Schubring, *Die italienische Plastik des Quattrocento*, Berlin, 1919, p. 244; Lorenzetti, [1]1926, p. 543; Gallo, *op. cit.*, *Rivista di Venezia*, 1926, p. 485 (with reservations); Mariacher, *Le arti*, 1940–41, p. 196; *idem*, *Arte veneta*, 1948, pp. 72f.; *idem*, *BM*, 1950, p. 127 (with the collaboration and under the influence of Bregno), and other places; Pope-Hennessy, *Ital. Ren. Sc.*, [1]1958, p. 349; Michelangelo Muraro, "La Scala senza Giganti," *De artibus opuscula XL. Essays in Honor of Erwin Panofsky*, ed. Millard Meiss, Zurich, 1960, i, p. 362; Romanini, *Arte lombarda*, January–June 1964, pp. 91ff.; Zava Bocazzi, *SS. Giovanni e Paolo*, 1965, p. 96; Pincus, *op. cit.*, *Art Bulletin*, 1969, p. 250; Zorzi, *Ven. scomparsa*, 1972, i, p. 135; Pincus, 1974, p. 311.

96. Planiscig, *VB*, 1921, pp. 36, 64, pointing to analogies

between *St. Helen* and the *Foscari Virtues* and the portrait of *Capello* and the *Effigy* of the doge, assigned the tomb to the shop, if not the hand, of Antonio Bregno. He noted further that between the statues from the Capello Tomb and those of Rizzo's Tron Tomb or his *Adam* and *Eve* there existed very little agreement. However, his appreciation of the similarities between *St. Helen* and the three *Virtues* from the Giustiniani Tomb, of whose existence he subsequently learned and of whose attribution to Rizzo he was easily convinced, necessitated Planiscig's reassessment of his attribution of the Capello Tomb. In *VJ*, 1926, pp. 97f., Planiscig replaced the name of Bregno by that of Rizzo. Yet he did not exclude the possibility of the intervention of assistants in the Capello Tomb. In 1934, Planiscig, T-B, xxviii, p. 409, reiterated his belief in Rizzo's authorship. Guyer, *Venice, Buildings and Sculptures*, 1928, p. xix, adopted Planiscig's initial attribution of the tomb to Bregno. Fiocco, *Dedalo*, 1927–28, p. 454, related the Capello Tomb to the Foscari Tomb which he attributed to Antonio and Paolo Bregno. In "Rizzo, Antonio," *Enciclopedia italiana*, Milan, xxix, 1936, p. 502, Fiocco espoused the orthodox attribution to Rizzo.

97. Ignoring the stylistic links between the Capello Tomb figures and the Foscari Tomb, but realizing that the author of the portrait of *Capello* could not have executed *Adam*, Pohlandt, *BJ*, 1971, pp. 202f., found it most convenient to reintroduce Dentone's name. (Confusing the issue, McAndrew, *op. cit.*, *Art Bulletin*, 1969, p. 25, n. 44, had asserted that Rizzo and Dentone were associated on the execution of the tomb.) Wolfgang Wolters, "Eine Antikenergänzung aus dem Kreis des Donatello in Venedig," *Pantheon*, xxxii, 1974, pp. 131, 133, n. 11, seconded Pohlandt's removal of the Capello Tomb from Rizzo's oeuvre, but refused to give its author another name.

98. Romanini, *Arte lombarda*, January–June 1964, p. 92; Pohlandt, *BJ*, 1971, p. 203; Munman, *BM*, 1971, p. 145. Pozzi, *op. cit.*, *Revue numismatique*, 1914, p. 206, traced *Capello*'s features to the plaquette he found with Capello's portrait.

99. Palazzo Ducale negative numbers: 5265 (=1850); 5268 (=1854); 5269 (=1853).

100. Giovanni Mariacher, "Di alcune sculture della 'Madonna dell'Orto'," *Ateneo veneto*, cxxxi, 1940, pp. 155f., attributed the figure to Matteo Raverti, hypothesizing that it had been made for an older main portal. Mariacher reiterated this opinion in "Aggiunta a Matteo Raverti," *Rivista d'arte*, xxii, 1940, pp. 102ff. (where the statue was dated between 1399 and 1420); *idem*, "Sculture di Castiglione Olona," *L'arte*, xlv,

1942, p. 60; *idem*, "Appunti per un profilo della scultura gotica veneziana," Venice. Istituto di scienze, lettere ed arti. *Atti* (Classe di scienze morali e lettere), cix, 1950–51, p. 244, and in other articles. In *Diz. bio.*, xii, 1970, p. 276, Mariacher wrote less confidently of the authorship of the statue, calling it a "prodotto tipicamente lombardo-ravertiano." Mariacher's attribution and dating have been adopted only by Maria Cionini Visani, "Proposta per Matteo Raverti," *Arte veneta*, xvi, 1962, pp. 35, 41, n. 8.

101. Pietro Antonio Pacifico, *Cronica veneta, overo succinto racconto di tutte le cose più cospicue, & antiche della Città di Venetia*, Venice, 1697, p. 336; Francesco Maria Tassi, *Vite de' pittori scultori e architetti bergamaschi*, Bergamo, 1793, i, p. 21 (who, however, confused the 15th-century Bartolomeo Bon and the 16th-century Bergamasque architect of the same name); Johann Christoph Maier, *Beschreibung von Venedig*, Leipzig, pt. 1, 1795, pp. 338f.; Moschini, 1815, ii, pp. 9f.; Paoletti, *Il fiore*, iii, 1840, p. 27; Alessandro Zanetti, "Buono, Bartolomeo," *Enciclopedia italiana, o dizionario della conversazione*, Venice, iv, 1841, p. 1339 (although confusing the two Bons); Selvatico, *Sulla architettura*, 1847, p. 137; Burckhardt, *Cic.*, ¹1855, p. 620b; Zanotto, *Nuovissima guida*, 1856, p. 325 (Bartolomeo Buono II); Vincenzo Zanetti, *La chiesa della Madonna dell'Orto in Venezia*, Venice, 1870, pp. 49ff. (Bartolomeo Buono I); Paoletti, 1893, i, p. 55; Lorenzetti, ¹1926, p. 395 (with reservations); Giuseppe Bigaglia, *La chiesa della Madonna dell'Orto in Venezia*, Venice, 1937, pp. 9, 10; Gallo, *Atti Ist. ven.*, 1961–62, p. 200; Pincus, 1974, p. 370; Susan Connell, *The Employment of Sculptors and Stonemasons in Venice in the Fifteenth Century*, Ph.D. dissertation, University of London, Warburg Institute, London, 1976 (typescript), p. 19.

Venturi, *Storia*, vi, 1908, pp. 994, 1061, was the first to cast doubt upon the attribution to Bon. Without specifically naming the *St. Christopher*, he assigned all the statues of the portal to that anonymous archaizing companion of Antonio Rizzo, whose style was characterized by "panni bagnati e strizzati," responsible for *St. Helen* from the Capello Tomb, the figures of the *Annunciation* from the Foscari Tomb, and the statues above the lunette of the portal of the Scuola di S. Marco. Bouchaud, *La sculpture vénitienne*, 1913, p. 87, plagiarized Venturi. In his review of the material, Paoletti, "Bono," T-B, iv, 1910, p. 316, suggested that *St. Christopher* might have been completed by an assistant in Bon's shop. Influenced by Paoletti's revision, Venturi, *Storia*, viii, pt. 2, 1924, pp. 315f., attributed all three portal statues to a pupil of Bon's.

102. Sansovino, 1581, p. 59r: "Nella facciata [of the Madonna dell'Orto] appariscono 13. figure di marmo, delle quali la migliore posta su la porta grande in mezzo, fu scolpita da Bartolomeo [Bon] che fece la porta di Palazzo."

103. Gallo, *Atti Ist. ven.*, 1961–62, pp. 203f., docs. ii, iii.

104. See A. M. Schulz, *op. cit.*, *Transactions of the American Philosophical Society*, in press.

105. "L'ultrasuono pulisce Venezia," *Il Giorno* (Milan), xiv, no. 215, September 16, 1969, p. 6.

106. *Le arti*, 1940–41, p. 197. Most of the analyses of the style of the *Virgin* take as their point of departure the observations made by Venturi, *Storia*, vi, 1908, pp. 994, 1061, discussed above, n. 101. Fiocco, *Enc. ital.*, xxix, 1936, p. 502, linked the figures of the *Virgin* and *Angel* to works by Antonio Bregno, yet he attributed them to Rizzo. Mariacher, *Le arti*, 1940–41, p. 196, and *idem*, *Arte veneta*, 1948, pp. 68, 72, perceived analogies between the *Annunciate Virgin* and *Angel*, on the one hand, and the *Foscari Annunciation* and the Capello *St. Helen*, on the other. This justified for him an attribution of the figures to Antonio Rizzo. That attribution was approved by Arslan, *op. cit.*, *Gazette des beaux-arts*, September 1953, p. 107, and Romanini, *Arte lombarda*, January–June 1964, p. 92, who referred again to a relationship between the *Virgin* and *St. Helen*. That relationship was stressed also by Pohlandt, *BJ*, 1971, p. 204, who, in addition, noted resemblances between the drapery of *Mary* and that of the *Virtues* of the Foscari Tomb. Although Paoletti, 1893, i, p. 55, recognized long ago that the *Annunciate Virgin* and *Angel* were executed by different sculptors, none of the aforementioned scholars explicitly distinguishes between the styles of the two figures.

107. In contrast to the Florentines, Venetian painters, especially Giovanni Bellini, preferred to show St. Jerome reading, not beating his breast in penitence. See Millard Meiss, "Scholarship and Penitence in the Early Renaissance: The Image of St. Jerome," *Pantheon*, xxxii, 1974, p. 138.

108. For the passage from this letter which applies to our relief see *Sancti Eusebii Hieronymi epistulae*, pt. 1, ed. I. Hilberg (Corpus scriptorum ecclesiasticorum Latinorum, liv), Vienna/Leipzig, 1910, pp. 152ff., letter xxii, par. 7. Acquaintance with this passage of St. Jerome's letter to Eustochium was widely diffused through its quotation by Jacopo da Voragine in his *Legenda*

aurea composed before 1264 (ch. cxliv, September 30). The entire letter was translated into Italian by the Dominican Domenico Cavalca (d. 1342). For a recent treatment of the iconography of St. Jerome see especially Renate Jungblut, *Hieronymus: Darstellung und Verehrung eines Kirchenvaters*, dissertation, Eberhard-Karls-Universität, Tübingen, 1967, esp. pp. 137ff.

109. Johannes Andreae, *Hieronymianus*, Cologne, 1482, n.p. [p. 18]: "dictavi formam quae nunc in cathedra sedens pingitur cum capello. quo nunc cardinales utuntur deposito ex leone mansueto. sic in publico domus proprie plene ipsius historiam feci depingi."

110. Jacopo Bellini also included a dragon (a favorite motif of his), a lion, and other animals in representations of St. Jerome. See Victor Goloubew, *Les dessins de Jacopo Bellini au Louvre et au British Museum*, Brussels, i, 1912, pl. xix; ii, 1908, pls. xiv, xxi. From Bellini's drawings the motif of the dragon also migrated to Venetian painting: see, for instance, Carlo Crivelli's predella panel with the penitent St. Jerome, National Gallery, London.

111. Susan Donahue Kuretsky, "Rembrandt's Tree Stump: An Iconographic Attribute of St. Jerome," *Art Bulletin*, lvi, 1974, pp. 571ff.

112. I am grateful to Mr. Anthony Radcliffe of the Victoria and Albert Museum for this information.

113. The first mention of the relief dates only from 1926: Lorenzetti, [1]1926, p. 489: "lombardesco (fine XV sec.)." At that time the relief was immured in the wall immediately to the right of the main entrance in the church of S. Maria del Giglio. Standing directly in front of it, largely concealing it from view, was Giulio dal Moro's statue of the *Redeemer*. The relief remained in this position after the recent restoration of the church, but the statue of the *Redeemer* was moved to one side.

114. Planiscig, "Deux reliefs en marbre de Pietro Lombardi," *Gazette des beaux-arts*, series 6, lxxii, pt. 1, January 1930, pp. 1ff., esp. p. 6. The attribution to Pietro Lombardo was reiterated by Planiscig, "Pietro, Tullio und Antonio Lombardo. (Neue Beiträge zu ihrem Werk.)," *Jahrbuch der kunsthistorischen Sammlungen in Wien*, n.F. xi, 1937, pp. 94f. Cognizance of Planiscig's attribution was taken by: Mario Brunetti, *S. Maria del Giglio vulgo Zobenigo nell'arte e nella storia*, Venice, 1952, pp. 22f.; Lorenzetti, [3]1963, p. 519; Hubala in Egg *et al.*, *Oberitalien Ost*, [1]1965,

p. 903. They neither dispute nor concur in the attribution.

115. Cvito Fisković, "Radovi Nikole Firentinca u Zadru," *Peristil*, iv, 1961, pp. 69f.; *idem*, "Naše umjetničke veze s južnom Italijom," *Mogućnosti* (Split), viii, no. 12, December 1961, p. 1231; *idem*, "Alešijev reljef u Londonu," *Peristil*, x–xi, 1967–68, p. 47; *idem*, "Iz nepoznate riznice: Neobjavljeni reljef Andrije Aleši-ja," *Telegram* (Zagreb), ix, no. 455, January 17, 1969, p. 17. Ivo Petricioli, "Prilog Alešijevoj i Firentinčevoj radionici," *Prilozi povijesti umjetnosti u Dalmaciji* (Split), xv, 1963, pp. 68ff., 74, introduced the name of Niccolò Fiorentino in connection with the Venetian relief without quite committing himself to an attribution. Vladimir Gvozdanović, "Prilog radionici Nikole Firentinca i Andrije Alešija," *Peristil*, x–xi, 1967–68, p. 63: close to the Aleši-Fiorentino shop.

116. Mothes, *Geschichte*, i, 1859, p. 288, long ago observed that the Foscari Tomb was the product of a very young sculptor.

II # Attribution of the Venetian Works

THE FOLLOWING CANDIDATES have been proposed for the authorship of one or more of the works discussed in chapter one: Bartolomeo Bon, Matteo Raverti, Antonio Dentone, Antonio Bregno, Antonio Rizzo, and Andrea Aleši. None provides a satisfactory solution. That Bartolomeo Bon could not be responsible for these works we believe to be established by our reconstruction of his artistic personality in another place[1] where an examination of his documented works, and a reconsideration of the repute which the sculptor enjoyed between 1445 and 1460 permit the reconstitution of a stylistically coherent oeuvre. That oeuvre consists of the two subordinate but artistically progressive angels on the lintel of the portal of the Scuola Vecchia della Misericordia executed by Bartolomeo in 1424 as an assistant of his father; the wellhead of the Ca' d'Oro of 1427–28; the *Fortitude* and *Temperance* from the inscribed and documented Porta della Carta (ca. 1442); the undocumented *S. Alvise* from the Venetian church of that name (1450s?); the statue of *Arithmetic* from the Arco Foscari (early 1460s); and the commencement of the group of the *Annunciation* in the Victoria and Albert Museum, London, possibly intended for the portal of the Madonna dell'Orto. Our survey of Bartolomeo's oeuvre reveals an artist who, on the one hand, was artistically formed in the Gothic style and strongly influenced in his youth by the new International Style, yet on the other, assimilated Renaissance discoveries in the rendering of anatomy and movement, in the logical explication of drapery patterns, in the adaptation of sculpture to specific points of sight—an artist, in sum, who represented in Venice that stage in the development of Renaissance style exemplified in Florence by Ghiberti.

As the author of our Venetian works the Lombard Matteo Raverti, active at the Duomo of Milan in the last decade of the fourteenth century and the first decade of the fifteenth century and documented at Venice from 1421 to 1436, need not be taken seriously. Clearly the works discussed, including the *St. Christopher* which Mariacher believed transferred from an earlier portal, are the work of a sculptor trained in the 1440s and not around 1390. Moreover, nothing whatever links the style of these works with that of the only certain sculpture by Raverti, the statue of *St. Babila* from the Duomo of Milan. Nor is Antonio Dentone an acceptable alternative. Although Sansovino called him "scultore Viniziano di gran nome al suo tempo," his existence has never been verified by inscription or document, either in or outside Venice. Therefore later students of Venetian sculpture, properly skeptical of his existence, supposed that Sansovino mistook him for Antonio Rizzo, whom they preferred to view as author of the Giustiniani and Capello Tombs.[2] Although I do not believe that Rizzo was responsible for either tomb, I think it likely that Dentone is an invention of Sansovino's.

Why are students of Venetian sculpture not equally skeptical of the existence of Antonio Bregno? To Bregno the Foscari Tomb is universally attributed, serving as a touchstone for the attribution to him of many other works. Some of these, such as *Music*, *Rhetoric*, the *Gorgon Warrior*, and *St. Mark* from the Arco Foscari, are by the master of the Foscari Tomb or his assistants, but most of them are not.[3] Presented with an oeuvre, Bregno has also been blessed with a biography. Born in Como, Bregno supposedly was trained in Lombardy by Matteo Raverti. By 1425 he had emigrated to Venice where, in that and the following year, he worked at the Ca' d'Oro under the supervision of Raverti.[4] Bregno later became the teacher of Antonio Rizzo, who made his debut as an apprentice in Bregno's shop,[5] contributing figures to the crowning of the Foscari Tomb and the Arco Foscari and in 1483 succeeding Bregno, after the latter's death,[6] as *protomaestro* of the Ducal Palace.

The attribution of the Foscari Tomb to Antonio Bregno derives from the inscription of Giampiccoli's rather free engraving of the tomb of 1777 in which the tomb is said to be the "opera d'invenzione dissegno, e Travaglio dell'Architetto Paulo, e dello Scultore Antonio Frattelli Bregno di Como."[7] In his own Venetian guidebook published two years later, however, Giampiccoli omitted the attribution, betraying perhaps a certain doubt of its validity.[8] Nevertheless, in 1839 Zanotto conjectured that the information contained in the engraving had been derived from family documents.[9] Zanotto's assumption has never been challenged, although no inscription, signature, or document confirming Antonio or Paolo Bregno's authorship of the tomb, or indeed, proving their existence, has ever come to light.[10]

The name Antonio Bregno makes its first appearance in 1581 in *Venetia citta nobilissima* where Sansovino attributes to Antonio Bregno the east wing of the *cortile* of the Ducal Palace with the doge's apartment and the Scala dei Giganti, and the Tomb of Doge Niccolò Tron in S. Maria dei Frari.[11] (The Foscari Tomb, directly opposite the Tron Tomb in the choir of the church, immediately precedes the Tron Tomb in Sansovino's guide, but Sansovino does not assign it any author.[12]) Now it so happens that the east wing of the *cortile* of the Ducal Palace and the Scala dei Giganti are securely documented works by Antonio Rizzo, *protomaestro* of the Ducal Palace from 1484 until his flight from Venice in 1498.[13] The style of *Prudence* on the Tron Tomb—analogous to that of *Eve* from the Arco Foscari—makes Rizzo's participation in the execution of that monument also virtually certain. Clearly, then, Sansovino simply called Antonio Rizzo, Antonio Bregno. Indeed, Antonio Rizzo's name never appears in Sansovino's book. Even Rizzo's *Adam* and *Eve*, the latter of which is inscribed "ANTONIO · RIZO" on its base, was given by Sansovino to the Paduan sculptor Andrea Riccio.[14] The source of this misinformation was Vasari's *Vite*.[15] Since Riccio is the Italian form of the Venetian Rizzo (meaning curly-haired), the mistake is understandable in the commentary of someone not intimately acquainted with Venetian art. But that Sansovino did not correct Vasari's error is explicable only by Sansovino's ignorance of any artist by the name of Rizzo.

What is the source of the name Antonio Bregno? It is possible that Vasari's and Sansovino's conflation of Antonio Rizzo and Andrea Riccio prompted a further conflation, for the name Andrea followed by the surname Bregno and the birthplace Como (added in Giampiccoli's engraving) occurs on the epitaph in S. Maria sopra Minerva, Rome, of the approximately contemporaneous sculptor Andrea Bregno, which states that he was born in the town of Osteno in the diocese of Como.[16] The hypothesis of Sansovino's triple conflation of Antonio Rizzo, Andrea Riccio, and Andrea Bregno receives support from Paolo Giovio (1484–1552) of Como who evidently did confuse Antonio Rizzo and Andrea Bregno, calling Rizzo his compatriot[17] when all extant documents prove that Rizzo was born at Verona[18] and Riccio was born at Trent.[19] Thus not one piece of unobjectionable testimony can be adduced in favor of the existence of a late fifteenth-century sculptor called Antonio Bregno da Como, and we are obliged to renew our search for the author of the Tomb of Doge Francesco Foscari.

Antonio Rizzo is almost invariably credited with the Capello Monument and the Giustiniani Tomb. Evidence most often cited is the identity of the sarcophagus and bier in the Tron and Giustiniani Tombs. The analogy is indeed compelling, but we must explain it by Rizzo's imitation of someone else's composition, for every other stylistic index points to diverse authors. Even Grevembroch's drawing of the *Giustiniani Effigy* (Fig. 47) suffices to reveal a style very different from that of the *Effigy of Tron*. Where *Giustiniani*'s cloak falls into a few long parallel, gently curving folds, precisely like the cloak of *Foscari* (Fig. 31),

Tron's *manto* produces a flat mosaic of innumerable small, semitriangular creases made by low, irregular ridges densely crisscrossing one another. Munman has attributed the *Tron Effigy* to Antonio Rizzo.[20] His attribution is confirmed by the reappearance of this type of drapery in the figures from the Altars of SS. Clemente, Jacopo, and Paolo (Fig. 70) in S. Marco, established as products of Rizzo's shop by a recently discovered document of 1469.[21] Here, too, surfaces are uniformly blanketed by low, wavering ridges of small, irregularly shaped folds in disarray. The same drapery style characterizes the so-called *Mars* in the Ducal Palace whose stylistic—if not qualitative—relationship to Rizzo's *Adam* is indisputable. The face of *Adam* finds no analogy in the work of our master. The morphology of the hand he lays upon his breast is unlike *Capello*'s. The countenance of Rizzo's *Eve* (Fig. 72), with its smooth oval contour which incorporates an excessively receding and dimpled chin, with its extremely bulbous forehead and recessive inverted V-shaped hairline, is very different even from that head which resembles it most closely, the head of *Prudence* from the Foscari Tomb (Fig. 20). The long, corkscrew curls, which are a hallmark of Rizzo's female type, never appear in the works connected with our master.

Yugoslav art historians customarily attribute to Andrea Aleši[22] the relief of *St. Jerome* in S. Maria del Giglio. In support, they cite the altar of the hermit church of St. Jerome on Marjan inscribed with Aleši's name and the date of 1480 (Fig. 74).[23] Comparable in iconography and composition to the relief of *St. Jerome* in S. Maria del Giglio (Fig. 66), its quality is conspicuously inferior. Exploration of a particular psychological state evident in the Venetian saint's bowed posture and the woeful expression of his emaciated face contrasts with the straightforward presentation of a reading figure. The upper torso of the Marjan St. Jerome is turned forward nearly into frontal view: the obliquity produced in the Venetian St. Jerome by means of the foreshortening attendant upon a three-quarter view is produced here by a simple tilt. The strangely elongated neck is attached, like a piece of piping, to the chest and head. The flexion of the wrist and fingers and of the attenuated leg and foot confutes the existence of a bony structure. For the asymmetrical, syncopated and encompassing rhythms of the folds produced by the drapery of the Venetian St. Jerome, there is substituted the monotonous pattern of an equilateral triangle composed of one large catenary curve over the chest and two smaller curves over the legs whose parabolas are identical to one another and similar to the larger one above. Aleši does not set his animals and figures within deep wells whose rims, sometimes echoing the shape of the figure contained within, narrowly and completely enclose them. Where the Venetian St. Jerome is absorbed into the depths of his ovum-shaped grotto, St. Jerome at Marjan is held, as though by pincers, by the opening of the cave calligraphically subdivided into brackets. One might legitimately object that such differences are attributable to the decade at least which separates the works, but, in fact, with the exception of the more natural proportions of its figure, Aleši's relief of *St. Jerome* of ca. 1467 in the Baptistry at Trogir (Fig. 73) differs no less than the relief in Venice. Indeed, it furnished the model for the Marjan relief.[24]

Nevertheless, there are similarities to be reckoned with. Thematically, the three sculptures at Venice, Marjan, and Trogir are identical. The unusual motif of the dragon emerging from a hollow as well as the lion and the cardinal's hat have been included in all. The pose and position of the saint are similar. The technical problems posed by the medium, in spite of the larger scale of the Baptistry relief, have been solved analogously. All three are thick reliefs, excavated deeply. Limbs and other objects are carved in the round wherever possible; where impossible, forms are undercut. Given the fact, abundantly proved by his documented works, that Aleši was a mediocre and eclectic sculptor who, like those creatures which instinctively adopt the coloration of their ambient, naturally worked in the style of which- ever master employed him or was artistically preeminent, we may assume that Aleši was the borrower and not the lender, and that the source of Aleši's style were the works executed by our master. Whoever that may have been, he must have become known to Aleši while Aleši was involved in the construction of the Baptistry at Trogir, for, where the interior relief of *St. Jerome* (Fig. 73) betrays his influence, the exterior relief of the *Baptism of Christ* is still carved in the style and technique of Aleši's first master, Giorgio da Sebenico. Now there is ample evidence to show, not only that throughout the latter part of his career Aleši's art was dominated by that of his sometime partner, Niccolò di Giovanni Fiorentino, but that Aleši became acquainted with the work of Niccolò precisely during the construction of the Baptistry to whose internal frieze of twenty-six genii bearing garlands, Niccolò contributed two of his own and finished or reworked seven others by Aleši.[25]

The identification of our master with a sculptor active in Dalmatia is corroborated by two further reliefs of *St. Jerome*. One is a copy of the relief in S. Maria del Giglio to which a base, meant to incorporate the owner's coat of arms, was appended (Fig. 76).[26] Made of the same Brač stone, the dimensions of the narrative scene are practically identical to those at Venice.[27] Currently in the office of the Society of Friends of Ragusan Antiquities at Dubrov- nik, it comes from the Ragusan church of the Madonna of Kaštela where it was immured in the wall as "spoglia."[28] Although its surface is more worn than the relief in Venice and portions are mutilated, it manifests no decline in quality. The second relief, recently purchased by the Walker Art Gallery at Liverpool (Fig. 75), also seems to have a Dal- matian provenance.[29] Thematically, the relief accords with the relief of *St. Jerome* at S. Maria del Giglio (Fig. 66). The pose and action of the saint are different, but his physique is not. In both reliefs the figure is extremely robust and muscular. The dolicocephalic head is thrust forward on a long neck, accentuating the curvature of the spine. In both, the long locks, which cling to the skull as though they were wet, wave forward on the nape. The flat face with its high forehead and long triangular beard on which the locks are lightly etched is morphologically identical. The bony knees, the excessively protuberant shin bone, even the oddly shaped toes, are virtually the same. The rise and fall of the border of the garment over the projecting knees were inspired by the saint's counterpart in Venice. The technique of the strapwork folds of the Arco Foscari *St. Mark* (Fig. 35) is strikingly like that of the Liverpool *St. Jerome*. Its diversity of style from the *St. Jerome* in Venice and its lesser quality disprove an attribution to our master of the Liverpool relief. It is probably by Andrea Aleši to whom it is currently assigned and who, along with Niccolò di Giovanni, was most importantly active in Trogir when the relief is likely to have been made.[30] For the arms in the lower frame of the relief—the crowned doubleheaded eagle with spread wings, around whose neck is hung a quartered shield—and the initials, "A L," belonged to the Venetian Alvise Lando who, in the name of Venice, exercised supreme authority at Trogir from 1470 to 1472. Identical arms and initials embellish the relief of the Loggia di Giustizia at Trogir, dated by inscription to November 15, 1471, and attributed to Niccolò di Giovanni and his shop.[31]

Although but a hundredth its size and barely sketched, the face of St. Jerome from the relief at S. Maria del Giglio (Fig. 67) is morphologically similar to that of *God the Father* above the arch over the central apse of the Cathedral at Šibenik (Fig. 84) executed during the tenure as *protomaestro* of Niccolò di Giovanni, with whose works its style accords.[32] In both, the face is extraordinarily long and the features are set well below the middle line. The high forehead bulges below the hairline but recedes at the temples. The beetling brows are set immediately above the eyes. The very narrow mouth curves downward, and the moustache droops around the corners of the mouth. The high and widely spaced cheekbones accent the emaciated cheeks, while the beard—an elongated triangle with blunted nadir—endows the lower halves of both faces with rigorously diagonal contours. Another example of this physiognomy occurs in the head of the mourning man at the rear of the relief of the *Lamentation over the Dead Christ* in the church of St. John the Baptist in Trogir (Fig. 80). Both here and in St. Jerome the head of hair possesses an independent mass whose uneven surface and gradual disappearance at the forehead prevent it from resembling a wig. In both, the withdrawal of the hairline leaves exposed an inordinate amount of brow and skull. On the head of hair are lightly incised short, irregular, and broken lines which produce no perceptible pattern but endow the hair with a fine and silken texture. The embedding of the tiny ear within the matrix of the head, as though within a socket, contributes to the straight diagonal contour of the jaw.

Though undocumented, the relief of the *Lamentation over the Dead Christ* (Figs. 77–80) possesses the best claim to recognition as an autograph work of Niccolò's.[33] In quality, it ranks with works by Donatello; in dramatic pathos it rivals contemporary *Lamentation* groups by Niccolò dell'Arca and Guido Mazzoni. The relief is known to have come from the altar of the Cippico family in the Benedictine church of St. John the Baptist in Trogir.[34] Probably the relief was commissioned by the Humanist historian Coriolano Cippico (1425– 93), for whose newly constructed palace in Trogir Niccolò carved two genii in the portal inscribed with Coriolano's name. It was Cippico who, as the sculptor's procurator, represented Niccolò at the signing of the contract for the Chapel of Beato Giovanni Orsini. Very likely the relief was begun soon after Niccolò's arrival in Trogir: the *Lamentation* from the Tomb of Giovanni and Simone Sobota in St. Dominic, Trogir (Fig. 92), inscribed 1469, is indebted to the relief. When, in the nineteenth century, the church of St. John the Baptist was disestablished and fell into disrepair, the *Lamentation* was moved to the city's cemetery. Around 1939 it was transferred to the lapidarium of Trogir installed in the former church.[35]

The drama of the *Lamentation* exceeds by far that of most of the other works attributed to Niccolò. Yet its drama differs only in degree—as, indeed, it should, given the nature of its theme—from the excitement generated by the figures of the Foscari Tomb. In both, the surging swathes of drapery, which possess a momentum of their own, convey the figures' charged emotional response. The seizure of that one least stable and most instantaneous phase from a continuum of movement, which characterizes the poses of the *Virtues* and *Warriors* from the Foscari Tomb, recurs in the frenzied figures of the *Lamentation* where the crouching or reaching figures exceed the range of possibilities of human movement, where no part of the body that is capable of bending or changing its direction is exempt from doing so, where even the digits of the hands and feet are animated.

The treatment of relief is identical to that of *St. Jerome* (Figs. 66, 78): both evoke a very strong sensation of a limited recession. Indeed, in both it would be more accurate to say projection than recession, for the background of the relief, located close to the foremost plane, is a solid and impenetrable wall before which forms spring forward with increasing force into the observer's space. Ordinarily, this type of composition characterizes reliefs modeled in wax or clay: a carver works inward from the front face of his block. As in the relief of *St. Jerome*, elements which occupy the rearmost plane of the relief, though flattened, are not squashed, and so far from being merely drawn upon the ground, are given boundaries of measurable depth which betray the solidity of the plane on which they lie. Nor is the solidity of that plane extenuated, as Donatello had done, by lightly incised clouds, or by any unevenness of surface destined to mottle the background with shadows. Indeed, in both, the surface of what is meant to figure as sky is not more highly polished than, or otherwise distinguished from, the surfaces of rocks, wooden crosses, or the ground on which the figures stand. In front of the background, elements are very densely overlapped: no illusion of empty space between successive layers of figures or landscape forms has been produced by a perspectival reduction in size or change in level. Figures or landscape forms which serve as foils to figures placed in front of them are represented frontally. Foremost figures are turned into three-quarter view and posed so that limbs, hands, and heads produce as many overlapping layers as can be extracted from the human figure. Heads, limbs, even swathes of drapery not only are carved in the round but are excavated from underneath so that they bridge abysses or emerge from wells of shadow. Foils made by limbs or drapery are invariably set far behind the object superposed. Thus, as we have seen before, the surface is subjected to constant and extraordinary dislocations producing an intense chiaroscuro.

Despite a diversity of expression and physical type, all the figures, but most noticeably Christ and the figure that touches the forehead of the Virgin (Figs. 77, 79), bear a family resemblance to *St. Christopher* (Fig. 63). Since the skull and forehead of all the figures are extremely high, the eyes occur at approximately the middle of the head and the features are compressed within the lower portion of the face. High above the brows a bulge traverses the entire forehead. Below, the temples recede sharply. Eyebrows press down upon deeply indented and widely spaced eyes. The brows would be absolutely straight were it not for the scarcely perceptible dip in the center of their contour. The eyebrows stretch considerably past the outer corners of the eyes where they accommodate a fleshy bulge. The eyeballs protrude and the lower orbit of the eye is clearly marked. Common to all the figures is the relatively short nose with its high bridge and small nostrils which hardly project beyond the slopes of the nose. The prominent cheekbones, high beneath the eyes, are located far to either side. Thus the front and rather flat plane of the face is extended almost to the face's lateral boundaries. Concave cheeks succeeded by convex jawbones repeat the sequence of indented temples and salient cheekbones and give a square shape to the face's silhouette. The chin is small. Inevitably the mouth is opened. Deeply hollowed, the corners of the mouth possess the rounded contour formed by a drill.

Niccolò di Giovanni's *Genius* on the left of the frieze above the lateral portal of Palazzo Cippico (Fig. 81)[36] wears a cloak tied like that of the Foscari Tomb *Prudence* (Fig. 16). Although here it is an outer rather than an inner border, the pattern produced by the right contour of the *Genius*'s cloak, with its sudden change of direction, is almost identical to that of the left border of *Prudence*'s cloak. It is an angle that Niccolò prefers and uses repeatedly—for example, in the half figure of *Charity* from the Foscari sarcophagus (Fig. 5) or in the mourning woman from the *Lamentation over the Dead Christ* (Fig. 78). The *Genius*'s graceful lowered hand, which seems devoid of a bony structure and incapable of exerting pressure, parallels the lowered hand of the *Annunciate Angel* from the Foscari Tomb (Fig. 29). There, too, the wrist bends very slightly. The long thumb, detached from the rest of the hand, curves upward. The index and middle fingers are spread apart in an inverted V. The middle and fourth fingers are parallel and contiguous throughout, while the long fifth finger is detached. Bent outward slightly at the second knuckle, it presses inward toward its termination against scroll or lily.

The right *Genius*'s extended hand recalls the opened hand of the *Foscari Charity* (Figs. 82, 5). In both, the back of the hand is plump and extremely short, both absolutely as well as in proportion to the long and narrow fingers. Where the fingers join the hand their circumference is narrowed. Their contours are predominantly straight: the fingers taper only at their tips. The fingernails are minute. The flexion of the joints is so gradual and surfaces are so smoothly and continuously rounded that hands seem to lack a bony framework. In both hands, the bowed little finger elegantly isolates itself from the straight fourth finger, depressed throughout its length. The unnaturalness of *Charity*'s gesture is augmented by the thumb turned forward, jutting straight out from the hand. The curving silhouette which this produces is accentuated by the swelling of the pad of the thumb and the tapering of its tip. This mannered treatment of the thumb is so prevalent among Niccolò's figures that it has come to be considered a hallmark of his, or his *bottega*'s work. As an example, it suffices to cite Niccolò's torch-bearing *Putto* from the dado of the Chapel of Beato Giovanni Orsini (Fig. 83).

The face of *Charity* (Fig. 3) is reminiscent of the faces of two marble *Angels*, probably by two different assistants of Niccolò, which originally embellished the lateral wings of a tabernacle, but which are now dispersed to either side of the first altar on the left of the Duomo at Šibenik (Figs. 85, 86).[37] In all three, tiny features are concentrated in the center of a wide face framed by a luxuriant mass of hair. *Charity*'s eyes, like those of the *Angel* on the right, are tiny and almond-shaped and very widely spaced. In both, the tear duct is suppressed. Although the eyes are barely recessed within the orbits of the eyes, the eyeballs are fairly protuberant. The brows arch high above the eyes; swellings beneath the brows are succeeded by long horizontal indentations aligned with the outer corners of the eyes. In both, the nose is extremely short and thin; the nostrils, tiny; and the bridge, extraordinarily contracted. All three heads exhibit an unusually narrow mouth and a round, blunt chin located immediately beneath the lower lip. The necks of *Charity* and the *Angel* on the left are extremely long and thick—rather too large in proportion to the heads. The tilt and turn of the two heads bestow upon the necks the same inorganically bowed contour, and in both, the pressure of the chin against the neck causes a double chin to form. *Charity*'s sash, with its uncommon form of knot (Fig. 5), reappears in the *Angel* on the left. The sash and knot were copied by a less able member of Niccolò's shop in the lamenting woman with upraised arms in the lunette relief of the Tomb of Giovanni and Simone Sobota (Fig. 92). To judge from her contracted mouth and tiny, widely spaced eyes, it was from *Charity*'s face, or one comparable to it, that he derived the features of his mourner.

The pattern of folds over the legs of the left *Angel* in the Duomo at Šibenik (Fig. 85) seems to have been inspired by that model which also influenced the figure of *Temperance* from the Giustiniani Tomb (Fig. 43). Although the author of the *Angel* was obliged to adapt a revolving design to a flat surface, he appropriated the long sweeping fold which diagonally traverses the left thigh, the foils of drapery against which both legs are seen, the configuration of breaking folds at the right knee and the adherence of the drapery to the shin below. In both, a wad of tightly clustered folds rolls over the arch of the right foot, leaving an identical amount of foot exposed. The lowered hands of the left *Angel* and the *Giustiniani Charity* (Fig. 42) are closely related—probably through a common source.

An unpublished statue of *St. John the Baptist* (Fig. 87) now in the lunette of the main portal of the church of St. John the Baptist in Šibenik reflects the pose, the gesture, and, to a lesser extent, the drapery of *Rhetoric* from the Arco Foscari (Fig. 41).[38] The statue, dwarfed by the lunette which, in any case, is later,[39] probably originally surmounted the balustrade which the Confraternity of S. Giovanni di Monte commissioned from Niccolò in 1475 to rail the external staircase along the church's southern flank.[40] The statue is badly damaged. At some unknown date its head was broken and was replaced by a much earlier one still Romanesque in style. The style of the statue justifies an attribution to Niccolò; its quality bespeaks the master's hand.

The unorthodox contrapposto of the *Baptist*, in which the weight seems almost equally distributed between free and engaged legs because the bent knee is represented frontally and the axis of the two knees is level, reproduces the pose of *Rhetoric* (Fig. 41). The poses of the arms are also similar. The mannered gesture of *Rhetoric*'s lowered hand with its markedly curving thumb and straightened elongated index finger has been given the significance of pointing in the *Baptist*. The pattern of *Rhetoric*'s drapery seems reflected in the oval swirl of folds on the *Baptist*'s stomach, in the diagonal fold descending from his hip, and in the foil of drapery behind his right thigh. The anatomy of the figure's bent leg—the extraordinary contraction of the knee turned forward, the exceptional bowing of the shin bone, and the bulging of the taut muscle just above the knee—is that exactly of the Venetian St. Jerome (Fig. 66).

Evidently it was from a figure by Niccolò very similar to this that the undated but probably earlier figure of *St. John the Baptist* carved by Andrea Aleši for the altar of the Baptistry at Trogir (Fig. 88) was drawn. We note with astonishment that the cloak of Aleši's *Baptist* derives from that of the right-hand *Warrior* of the Foscari Tomb (Fig. 12), and that the head of hair, though far less plastic, is composed of Niccolò's idiosyncratic tufts which, sprouting from the center of a high skull, fall to either side or flop forward on the forehead in discrete layers.

In the lions of the Tomb of Giovanni Sobota and his son, Simone, in St. Dominic, Trogir (Fig. 90), we see at work that process which had animated the *Virtues* of the Foscari Tomb, transforming them from passive symbols to active participants in a drama.[41] In the Sobota Tomb the sarcophagus no longer rests on rectangular slabs whose front face has been given the semblance of a lion as in Donatello's Coscia Tomb, but on lions as real as the *Foscari*

Virtues and as independent of the architecture of the tomb. Life-size, they are much larger in scale than any of the human figures on the tomb, and this, plus their unique plasticity and projection, make them seem much the most important element of the tomb. They are carved in the round in their entirety. The naturalness of their poses testifies to observation at first hand. The lion on the right, the only portion of the tomb for whose execution Niccolò himself was entirely responsible, is no less afflicted by his grief than the lamenters over the dead Christ in the lunette.

The over life-size statue of *St. James* above the east end of the Cathedral at Šibenik by an assistant of Niccolò (Fig. 89)[42] recalls the Arco Foscari *St. Mark* (Fig. 35). Common to both are the cloak draped over one shoulder and the triple swathe of drapery traversing abdomen, hips, and thighs. The swathe that encircles the figure's left ankle corresponds to the swathe that binds the lower legs of the *Foscari Christ* (Fig. 28). This motif, so very odd because folds by themselves would never accidentally form such a pattern, and if they did, the figure could not walk, reappears in the statue of *St. James* in the Orsini Chapel by another anonymous assistant of Niccolò (Fig. 91). The pattern of swirls made by the drapery covering the legs of the *Foscari Christ* and the Arco Foscari *St. Mark* is comparable to the pattern of folds in the cloak of Niccolò's *Resurrected Christ* in the same chapel (Fig. 94). Although the face of the *Resurrected Christ* (Fig. 93) betrays a harder, more linear, and more schematic treatment than the face of the *Foscari Christ* (Fig. 23)—understandable in view of the thirty-six years which separate the works[43]—the two heads are attributable to a single sculptor. The hair of the *Resurrected Christ* constitutes a more compact and uniform mass, but it is arranged with the same central part, and the same regular series of waves which, retreating symmetrically at the upper corners of the forehead, endow it with its rectangular shape. In both, the eyebrows are nearly level and are raised in each to the same degree above the small and widely separated eyes. Protuberant eyeballs pull forward upper lids. The openings of the downcast eyes are delineated similarly: the lower contour of the upper lid is drawn straight across the middle of the eye; the more sharply curving lower lid makes a sudden detour around the short, high tear duct. The mouths are rather narrow and the lips are parted slightly. In neither does the lower lip reach the corners of the mouth.

The anatomical distortions of *St. James*'s left hand (Fig. 91) recur in *St. Francis* on the Foscari sarcophagus (Fig. 8) where the figure holds his book, ornamented identically, with *St. James*'s gesture. The grip of *St. James*'s other hand, the retracted arm and the elbow turned outward slightly recall the right arm of the *Moro Warrior* from the Arco Foscari (Fig. 38).

The face of the *Putto* above the column dividing the niches of *SS. Philip* and *John the Evangelist* in the Orsini Chapel (Fig. 95)[44] resembles the faces of the *Christ Child* from the Madonna dell'Orto (Fig. 65) and the *Angel* from the Foscari Tomb (Fig. 33). A high broad forehead is common to all three. Brows, whose curvature is minimal, are hardly elevated above eyes opened wide and widely spaced. The upward curving nose is very short. The rotund cheeks swell most directly opposite the corners of the mouth, causing the mouth to seem embedded in the depression formed between them. Two indentations descend from either corner of the mouth almost to the lower contour of the face, while a third one, located at a considerable distance below the lower lip, sets the boundary of the very low but broad and protuberant chin.

Confirmation of our attribution of the Foscari Tomb and related monuments to Niccolò di Giovanni Fiorentino is to be found in an iconographic peculiarity of the Orsini Chapel not observed till now.[45] The entire chapel was conceived as a funerary monument commemorating Blessed Bishop Giovanni Orsini, the protector of Trogir, who had died in 1111. His effigy from a previous tomb surmounts the altar beneath which his bones lie. Behind the effigy, in the position of highest honor in the center of the rear wall of the chapel, in the niche now occupied by the *Resurrected Christ*, there originally stood an image of *Christ Ascending into Glory*. In the contract of January 4, 1468, with Aleši and Niccolò for the construction and decoration of the chapel, the group is described thus: "et fra li dicti apostoli de esser vno casamento de pie 7 a quadro et die esser quadrado, et nel casamento vna figura de Christo de piedi 5¼ et con el dicto Christo doi anzoleti a luj retegnudi de piedi doi l'uno. . . ."[46] Presumably this is the group for which Niccolò was paid in 1487.[47] The group is currently in the cemetery at Trogir (Fig. 96). It consists of a life-size standing figure of Christ flanked by two angels whose movement hints at flight. The haloless Christ is garbed, like the *Foscari Christ* (Fig. 28), in gown and cloak and thick-soled sandals. His pose—a moderated contrapposto in which the left foot advances slightly—is that of the *Foscari Christ*. Like its prototype, the figure blesses with his right hand and holds a closed book in his left. We do not know when the group of the *Ascending Christ* was moved from the chapel,[48] but presumably its removal predates 1494 when Niccolò was paid for a second statue of *Christ*. There has been much speculation on the cause of the alienation of the original group; most of it has focused on the style or condition of the group.[49] To be sure, its poor quality betrays the execution of an assistant. But it is no worse than several of the other statues in the chapel. The explanation for its removal is, rather, that the image of an *Ascending Christ* had potential relevance only in a Venetian ducal tomb: in any other funerary context it was heterodox. Of such theological subtleties Niccolò was probably unaware and argued on purely artistic grounds for the adoption of a scheme already used successfully in Venice. But his patrons were soon apprised of their mistake and replaced the *Ascension* seven years after its installation with the orthodox and conventional *Resurrection*.[50]

NOTES

1. "The Sculpture of Giovanni and Bartolomeo Bon and Their Workshop," *Transactions of the American Philosophical Society*, in press.

2. Paoletti, 1893, ii, pp. 144, 146; Venturi, *Storia*, vi, 1908, p. 1060; Antonio Muñoz in Ludwig Pollak and Muñoz, *Pièces de choix de la collection du Comte Grégoire Stroganoff. II. Moyen-âge, renaissance, époque moderne*, Rome, 1911, p. 117; Planiscig, *VJ*, 1926, p. 98; *idem*, T-B, xxviii, 1934, p. 408; Mariacher, *Arte veneta*, 1948, p. 69, n. 2; *idem*, "Due inedite sculture di Antonio Rizzo," *Rivista d'arte*, xxvii, 1951–52, p. 185; Munman, *BM*, 1971, p. 138; *idem*, "Antonio Rizzo's Sarcophagus for Nicolò Tron: A Closer Look," *Art Bulletin*, lv, 1973, pp. 77ff. Among recent scholars, only Pohlandt, *BJ*, 1971, pp. 200, 202, 204, has explicitly credited Dentone with an independent existence. To a certain extent her reasoning was sound: she realized that Rizzo was not the author of the Giustiniani and Capello Tombs and that therefore Dentone could not be Rizzo. But she made no attempt to find another, documented, author for the Giustiniani and Capello Tombs.

3. 1) The shield-bearing *Warrior* in the Museo Nazionale, Ravenna: Giovanni Mariacher, "Nota su due sculture veneziane al Museo Nazionale di Ravenna," *Felix Ravenna*, series 3, fasc. 6, December 1951, pp. 30f. 2) The *Annunciate Virgin* and *Angel*, Victoria and Albert Museum, London: Mariacher, *BM*, 1950, p. 124; Pope-Hennessy, *V & A Cat.*, 1964, i, pp. 346f.; Jolán Balogh, "Studi sulla collezione di sculture del Museo di Belle Arti di Budapest, vi, pt. 1, Pozzi veneziani," *Acta historiae artium*, xii, 1966, p. 245; *idem*, "Studi nella collezione di sculture del Museo di Belle Arti in Budapest, vii," *Acta historiae artium*, xv, 1969, p. 94; Budapest, Szépművészeti Múzeum, *Katalog der ausländischen Bildwerke des Museums der bildenden Künste in Budapest, iv.-xviii. Jahrhundert*, by Jolán Balogh, Budapest, 1975, i, p. 93, no. 105. 3) The *vera da pozzo* with the Testa arms, Szépművészeti Múzeum, Budapest, vii," *Acta historiae artium*, xv, 1969, p. 94; Budaartium, 1966, pp. 244ff.; *idem*, *op. cit.*, *Acta historiae artium*, xv, 1969, p. 94. 4) The *Archangel Gabriel* at the northwest corner of the Ducal Palace, Venice: Mariacher, *BM*, 1950, p. 124; Terisio Pignatti, *Palazzo Ducale Venezia*, Novara, 1964, p. 10. 5) The *Archangels Raphael* and *Michael* at the southeast and southwest corners of the Ducal Palace, respectively: *ibid.*,

p. 10. 6) *Fortitude* and *Temperance* from the Porta della Carta, Ducal Palace: Planiscig, *VB*, 1921, pp. 30ff.; Lorenzetti, ¹1926, p. 234; S. Guyer, *Venice, Buildings and Sculpture* (Mirabilia Mundi, 1), trans. L. B. Ellis, Augsburg, 1928, p. xix; Planiscig, *VJ*, 1930, p. 101; Géza de Francovich, "Bregno, Antonio," *Enciclopedia italiana*, Milan, vii, 1930, p. 792; Planiscig, T-B, xxviii, 1934, p. 409; Pope-Hennessy, *Ital. Goth. Sc.*, ¹1955, p. 224; Hubala in Egg *et al.*, *Oberitalien Ost*, ¹1965, p. 640; Arslan, *Ven. got.*, 1970, p. 253, n. 146; Wolfgang Wolters quoted in Venice. Procuratie Nuove. *Arte a Venezia dal medioevo al settecento*, June–October 1971, catalogue by Giovanni Mariacher, Venice, 1971, p. 134. (It is unclear here whether Wolters is referring to both *Virtues* or simply to *Fortitude*. In 1976 Wolters, i, pp. 124, 133, 284, 292, attributed with reservations only the figure of *Fortitude* to the master of the Foscari Tomb.) 7) *Charity* and *Prudence* from the Porta della Carta: Mariacher, *BM*, 1950, p. 124; Elena Bassi and Egle Renata Trincanato, *Il Palazzo Ducale nella storia e nell'arte di Venezia*, Milan, 1960, p. 44; Pignatti, *Palazzo Ducale Venezia*, 1964, p. 10. 8) The head of Doge Foscari from the Porta della Carta: Planiscig, *VB*, 1921, p. 36; Mariacher, *Pal. Duc.*, 1950, p. 23, fig. 21; *idem*, *BM*, 1950, p. 127; Pope-Hennessy, *Ital. Ren. Sc.*, ¹1958, p. 348; Ettore Belvedere, *Il Palazzo Ducale di Venezia*, Milan, 1960, p. 50. 9) The six worshiping youths at the base of the central pyramid and the worshiping youth next to *Prudence* on the Arco Foscari: Mariacher, *Le arti*, 1940–41, p. 194; *idem*, *Arte veneta*, 1948, p. 69; *idem*, *BM*, 1950, p. 127. 10) *Arithmetic*, Arco Foscari: Bassi and Trincanato, *Pal. Duc.*, 1960, p. 46.

4. Mariacher, *Le arti*, 1940–41, pp. 193ff.

5. This idea was first put forward by Fiocco, *Dedalo*, 1927–28, p. 454. It was adopted by Giovanni Mariacher, "Premesse storiche alla venuta dei lombardi a Venezia nel '400," Venice. Istituto di scienze, lettere ed arti. *Atti* (Classe di scienze morali e lettere), xcvii, pt. 2, 1937–38, p. 585, and has been repeated since in every article of his in which he deals with either Bregno or Rizzo. It surfaces also in Terisio Pignatti, *Piazza San Marco*, Novara, 1956, p. 30, and Egle Renata Trincanato, *Palazzo Ducale Venezia*, Novara, 1969, p. 9.

6. Mariacher, *op. cit.*, *Atti Ist. ven.*, 1937–38, p. 585; *idem*, *BM*, 1950, p. 127.

7. For a transcription of the entire legend see chapter 1, n. 29. For Marco Sebastiano Giampiccoli (1706-82) see Luigi Alpago-Novello, "Gli incisori bellunesi," Venice. Istituto di scienze, lettere ed arti. *Atti* (Classe di scienze morali e lettere), xcix, pt. 2, 1939-40, pp. 500-523, esp. p. 519.

8. [Marco Sebastiano Giampiccoli], *Notizie interessanti, che servono a far conoscere in tutti i suoi sestieri l'inclita città di Venezia*, Belluno, 1779, p. 79: ". . . accenneremo solo i Mausolei. Havvi quello del Doge Francesco Foscari nella Cappella maggiore ornato di belle figure di marmo. . . ."

9. Francesco Zanotto in Antonio Diedo and Zanotto, *I monumenti cospicui di Venezia*, Milan, 1839, n.p. [p. 27].

10. Several documents have been connected with Paolo and Antonio Bregno, but in none of them is either man ever called Bregno. The following documents have been linked with Paolo: in 1425 a "M.⁰ Paolo" was employed at the Ca' d'Oro under Matteo Raverti. (Paoletti, 1893, i, p. 21.) By October 27, 1460, a "M. paulo quale fa fare ognia lavorerio in Venexia per Sancto Marcho" had evaluated jointly with Bartolomeo Bon what had been erected of the Ca' del Duca. (Luca Beltrami, *La "Cà del Duca" sul Canal Grande ed altre reminiscenze sforzesche in Venezia* [per nozze Albertini-Giacosa], Milan, 1900, p. 22.) The following documents have been thought to refer to Antonio Bregno: three notices dated 1389, 1390, 1391, regarding a "Magistro Antonio da Regezia" employed by the *Fabbrica del Duomo* of Milan. (Ugo Nebbia, *La scultura nel Duomo di Milano*, Milan, 1908, index, p. 268.) In 1425 and 1426 an Antonio di Rigesio da Como was recorded at work at the Ca' d'Oro under Matteo Raverti. (Paoletti, 1893, i, pp. 21, 44; *idem*, "La Ca' d'Oro," in Venice. Museo Civico Correr. *Venezia, studi di arte e storia*, i, 1920, p. 98.) On May 12, 1449, an Antonio da Lugano living in Padua was credited by the *Arca del Santo* of Padua for several cornices and large stones to go inside and out on the altarpiece of the high altar being made by Donatello. (Antonio Sartori, "Documenti riguardanti Donatello e il suo altare di Padova," *Il Santo*, i, 1961, pp. 79, 81. See also a payment of June 22, 1449, to "maistro Antonio taiapria": *ibid.*, p. 81.) Clearly, no certainty attaches to the identification of Paolo or Antonio Bregno with any of the persons mentioned in these documents.

11. Sansovino, 1581, pp. 119v, 120r, 66r.

12. *Ibid.*, pp. 66vf.

13. Paoletti, 1893, ii, pp. 151f.

14. Anselmo Guisconi [Francesco Sansovino], *Tutte le cose notabili e belle che sono in Venetia*, Venice, 1556, n.p. [p. 6]; Sansovino, 1581, pp. 119rf.

15. *Le vite de piu eccellenti architetti, pittori, et scultori italiani* (from the edition of 1550), ed. Corrado Ricci, Milan/Rome, 1927, ii, p. 95; Giorgio Vasari, *Le vite de' più eccellenti pittori scultori ed architettori* (from the edition of 1568), ed. Gaetano Milanesi, Florence, ii, 1878, pp. 572f. The attribution of *Adam* and *Eve* to Andrea Riccio was also adopted by Bernardino Scardeone, *De antiquitate urbis Patavii & claris civibus Patavinis libri tres*, Basel, 1560, p. 375.

16. His epitaph begins: "ANDREAE BREGNO EX OSTEN AGRI COMENS / STATVARIO CELEBERIMO COGNOMENTO / POLYCLETO. . . ." The epitaph, which still exists, was published in Lorenz Schrader, *Monumentorum Italiae, quae hoc nostro saeculo et a Christianis posita sunt, libri quatuor*, Helmstadt, 1592, p. 155v. (It does not appear in the earlier editions of 1574, 1585, or 1589 of the book which were published at Breslau under the author and title of Tobias Fendt, *Monumenta sepulcrorum cum epigraphis ingenio et doctrina excellentium virorum*.) For an explication of the inscription see Hermann Egger, "Beiträge zur Andrea Bregno—Forschung," *Festschrift für Julius Schlosser*, Zurich/Leipzig/Vienna, 1927, pp. 128f.

17. Giovanni Battista Giovio, *Gli uomini della comasca diocesi antichi, e moderni nelle arti, e nelle lettere illustri*, Modena, 1784, p. 233, "Ricci, Andrea," quoting from an unpublished manuscript of Paolo Giovio: "Un Riccio nel contato all'età nostra / Nacque di Como, che fu buon scultore, / Et l'opre di costui Venetia mostra; / Fece un Adamo, ch'è di tal valore, / Che di bellezza cogli antichi giostra."

18. Paoletti, 1893, ii, p. 147.

19. Erice Rigoni, "Testamenti di tre scultori del Cinquecento," *Archivio veneto*, series 5, xxii, 1938, pp. 86f.

20. Munman, *op. cit.*, Art Bulletin, 1973, p. 81.

21. ASV, Cancelleria inferiore B. 212 (Notaio Tomaso de Tomasi), c. 8v: "1469 Mensis Junij die 28 indictione secunda, Rivoalti. Ser Antonius Rizo lapicida de confinio Sancti Johannis Novi cum heredibus et successoribus etc. suis rogavit securitatem illustrissimo et excellentissimo principi et domino domino Christoforo Mauro inclito duci Venetiarum et successoribus suis de ducatis XXXV auri pro resto et completa soluptione omnium laboreriorum per ipsum factorum circha tria altaria in ecclesia S. Marci et de omnibus et singulis quae quomodocumque agere secum habuit ab initio usque in presentem diem. Nunc autem etc.

Testes venerabilis presbiter Paulus Benedicto S. M.

Iubanico plebanus et cancellarius et Johannes Bernardus de Calleotis gastaldio."

Attention was first drawn to this document by Julia Helen Keydel, *A Group of Altarpieces by Giovanni Bellini Considered in Relation to the Context for which They Were Made*, Ph.D. dissertation, Harvard University, Cambridge, Mass., 1969 (typescript), p. 242, n. 15.

22. Born at Durrës (Durazzo) in Albania, Andrea di Niccolò Aleši is first documented in 1435 when he was apprenticed to Marco di Pietro da Troia at Zadar. (Giuseppe Praga, "Documenti intorno ad Andrea Alessi," *Rassegna marchigiana*, viii, 1929–30, p. 9, doc. 1.) Aleši can be traced in Šibenik in 1445 in the studio of Giorgio da Sebenico. (Pietro Gianuizzi, "Giorgio da Sebenico, architetto e scultore vissuto nel secolo xv," *Archivio storico dell'arte*, vii, 1894, p. 404.) In 1452 he assisted Giorgio in the execution of the figures and architectural details for the Loggia dei Mercanti at Ancona. (Frey-Molè, pp. 153f., doc. 98.) The destroyed Chapel of St. Catherine in St. Dominic at Split, based on Giorgio's Chapel of St. Rainerius, was commissioned in 1448 and was finished by 1453. (I. Kukuljević, "Aleksijev Andrija Dračanin," *Slovnik umjetnikah jugoslavenskih*, Zagreb, i, 1858, pp. 4f.; P. Kolendić, "Stube na crkvi sv. Ivana u Šibeniku," *Starinar* [Belgrade], series 3, i, 1923, p. 79, n. 69.) From 1453 to 1460 Aleši worked principally at, or for, Rab: documents record the following works: for Kolano Cernota the destroyed Chapel of SS. Jerome and Nicholas with an altar table and a balustrade and Cernota's extant tomb slab, all executed between 1453 and 1454 in the demolished church of St. John the Evangelist; the lost balustrade, altar table and tomb slab carved between 1454 and 1456 for the chapel of Niccolò Skafa also in St. John the Evangelist; the fragmentary Tomb slab of Bishop Giovanni Skafa and the extant balustrade in front of the Altar of St. Anastasia in the Cathedral of S. Maria Maggiore commissioned in 1454; also in the Cathedral, the destroyed chapel with its altar and holy water font constructed for Francesco Zudeniko between 1456 and 1460; the lost Tomb slab of Bishop Zudenik Zudeniko executed between 1454 and 1456 and located in the aforementioned chapel of Francesco Zudeniko; for Petar Car, two balustrades preserved in fragments, one for the apse of St. Bernardino at Kampor, the other for the Altar of Corpus Christi in the Cathedral, and Car's lost tomb slab for the former church, all commissioned in 1456 but not yet finished in 1458; a destroyed portal and window for the Palace of Zudenik Zudeniko commissioned in 1460 and probably finished in 1461. (Cvito Fisković, "Andrija Aleši i ostali majstori u Rabu," in Fisković and Kruno Prijatelj, *Albanski umjetnik Andri-*

ja Aleši u Splitu i u Rabu [Izdanje konzervatorskog zavoda za Dalmaciju u Splitu, 5], Split, 1948, pp. 13–44.) The Baptistry of the Cathedral of Trogir is inscribed with Aleši's name and the date of 1467. (See below, ch. 3, n. 4.) In 1468, together with Niccolò di Giovanni Fiorentino, he undertook the construction and decoration of the Chapel of Beato Giovanni Orsini in the Cathedral of Trogir on which work continued long after the death of both masters. (See Appendix, pp. 82ff.) For several years Aleši and Niccolò maintained a partnership, jointly repairing the Campanile of the Duomo of Split in 1472. (See Appendix, p. 85.) Together they erected the facade and sculptured portal of S. Maria on the island of S. Niccolò in the Tremiti archipelago in 1473. (See Appendix, pp. 86f.) The partnership apparently was terminated by Niccolò's nomination as *protomaestro* of the Cathedral at Šibenik upon the death of Giorgio da Sebenico. (See Appendix, p. 87.) From 1474 until his death, probably in the latter part of 1504, Aleši lived continuously at Split, executing works of stonemasonry and aiding in the construction of the fortifications of the city. A relief of *St. Jerome* with *SS John the Baptist* and *Anthony Abbot* on the altar of St. Jerome, Marjan, is inscribed and dated 1480. (See below, n. 23.) For Aleši's date of death see P. Kolendić, "Grob Andrije Alešija u Splitu," Skopsko naučno drustvo. *Glasnik* (Skopje), i, 1926, p. 491; Praga, *op. cit., Rassegna marchigiana*, 1929–30, p. 8; and Kruno Prijatelj, "Andrija Aleši u Splitu," in *Albanski umjetnik Andrija Aleši u Splitu i u Rabu*, 1948, p. 48. For Aleši's activity at Split see Praga, *op. cit., Rassegna marchigiana*, 1929–30, pp. 1–26 and 97–104; and Prijatelj, *op. cit.*, in *Albanski umjetnik Andrija Aleši u Splitu i u Rabu*, 1948, pp. 45–59.

23. "PBRO IOANNI DIVI HIERONIMI EMVLO · ANDREAS · LAPICIDA · DONO · MCCCCLXXX." This relief is discussed extensively by Prijatelj, *op. cit.*, in *Albanski umjetnik Andrija Aleši u Splitu i u Rabu*, 1948, pp. 45f. For the altarpiece in the context of the church for which it was made see Duško Kečkemet, "Crkvica i eremitaža sv. Jere na Marjanu," *Prilozi povijesti umjetnosti u Dalmaciji* (Split), xi, 1959, pp. 95ff., esp. p. 97.

24. Prijatelj, *op. cit.*, in *Albanski umjetnik Andrija Aleši u Splitu i u Rabu*, 1948, p. 46.

25. Cvito Fisković, "Aleši, Firentinac i Duknović u Trogiru," Jugoslavenska akademija znanosti i umjetnosti. Institut za likovne umjetnosti. *Bulletin* (Zagreb), vii, 1959, pp. 23f. (correcting an earlier attribution of three unspecified *putti* to Niccolò: *idem, Zadarski sredovječni majstori*, Split, 1959, pp. 54f.). In the later article Fisković attributed to Niccolò the following four *putti*: 1) the second on the north wall counting from the west; 2) the fourth on the east wall counting from

the north; 3) and 4) the fifth and sixth on the south wall counting from the west. In regard to the attribution of the first two *putti* I am in complete agreement. I would qualify Fisković's attribution of the latter two *putti* by suggesting that they were begun by Aleši and finished by Niccolò. In addition, I believe that Niccolò also participated, to a greater or lesser extent—mostly reworking parts already finished by Aleši—in the execution of the following *putti*: 1) the fifth on the east wall counting from the north; 2) the fourth on the west wall counting from the south; 3), 4), and 5) the fourth, fifth, and seventh on the north wall counting from the west.

26. The relief was first published by Kruno Prijatelj, "Novi prilog o Andriji Alešiju," *Prilozi povijesti umjetnosti u Dubrovniku*, vi, 1950, pp. 24f., who claimed it as a provincial revision of Aleši's model by a close assistant of his in the last decades of the 15th century. Prijatelj did not reject the possibility that Aleši himself might have contributed to the figure of St. Jerome. Ivo Petricioli, "Alešijev reljef sv. Jeronima u Zadru," *Vjesnik za arheologiju i historiju dalmatinsku*, lvi–lix, 1954–57 (*Zbornik radova posvećenih M. Abramiću*) (Split), pp. 272f., correctly noted the substantial difference that divided this from the reliefs of *St. Jerome* by Aleši or his shop at Marjan, Trogir, St. John at Zadar, the Gallery of Art at Split, and the Franciscan church at Kraj on the island of Pašman—a difference which indicated to Petricioli an "independent and much more confident sculptor." Cvito Fisković, "Radovi Nikole Firentinca u Zadru," *Peristil*, iv, 1961, p. 70: shop of Aleši. Ivo Petricioli, "Prilog Alešijevoj i Firentinčevoj radionici," *Prilozi povijesti umjetnosti u Dalmaciji*, xv, 1963, pp. 68ff., justly connected this and the relief in S. Maria del Giglio with a relief of *St. George and the Dragon* in St. George, Straževnik, on the island of Brač attributed to a close associate of Niccolò Fiorentino. Petricioli, *ibid.*, p. 74, asked provocatively whether Niccolò might not have "influenced the creation of this 'Alešian' type of composition of St. Jerome in the cave." Vladimir Gvozdanović, "Prilog radionici Nikole Firentinca i Andrije Alešija," *Peristil*, x–xi, 1967–68, pp. 63f.: close to the joint shop of Aleši and Fiorentino.

27. In its entirety the relief in Dubrovnik measures 40.5 cm. wide × 45.5 cm. high. The narrative scene, minus moldings and base, measures 36.5 cm. wide × 29 cm. high. The moldings are 2 cm. in width. The relief in S. Maria del Giglio measures 39.8 cm. wide × 31.5 cm. high including moldings.

28. Prijatelj, *op. cit.*, *Prilozi povijesti umjetnosti u Dubrovniku*, 1950, p. 24.

29. Cvito Fisković, "Alešijev reljef u Londonu," *Peristil*,

x–xi, 1967–68, pp. 47ff.; *idem*, "Iz nepoznate riznice: Neobjavljeni reljef Andrije Alešija," *Telegram* (Zagreb), ix, no. 455, January 17, 1969, p. 17; Liverpool, Walker Art Gallery. *Annual Report and Bulletin*, i, 1970–71, p. 13, no. 7278.

30. For Trogir's special devotion to St. Jerome in the 15th century see Ivo Delalle, "Sv. Jeronim u umjetnosti," *Kalendar "Jadran"* (Split), 1933, pp. 71–73.

31. Fisković, *op. cit.*, *Peristil*, 1967–68, p. 49.

32. See Appendix, pp. 87f.

33. No one who has ever written about this relief has doubted the attribution to Niccolò di Giovanni Fiorentino with the sole exception of Wolfgang Wolters, "Due capolavori della cerchia di Donatello a Trogir e a Šibenik," *Antichità viva*, vii, January–February 1968, pp. 11ff., who attributed it to an anonymous follower of Donatello. Wolters, however, seems not to have been acquainted with the copious literature on our artist in Serbo-Croatian. Wolters, *ibid.*, pp. 14f., erroneously assumed that the lamenting woman with upraised arms in Giorgio da Sebenico's Shrine of St. Rainerius at Kaštel Lukšić of 1444–48 must have been derived from the lamenting woman in our relief. This allowed him to postulate a *terminus ante quem* of 1448 for Niccolò's relief of the *Lamentation*. But the motif of the lamenting woman with upraised arms occurs in countless *Lamentations*: originating in Byzantine art, it appears in Italian painting already in the second half of the 13th century. Giorgio's lamenting woman, therefore, might have been derived from any number of sources. Indeed, the lamenting woman in the *Lamentation* from Duccio's *Maestà*, to choose at random one example, is closer to the lamenting woman in Giorgio's shrine than is the figure in Niccolò's relief. See Moshe Barasch, *Gestures of Despair in Medieval and Early Renaissance Art*, New York, 1976, pp. 60ff., 76f., 84. Wolter's thesis is also explicitly rejected by Cvito Fisković, "Neobjavljeno 'Oplakivanje' Jurja Dalmatinca," *Peristil*, x–xi, 1967–68, p. 45, n. 19.

34. Paolo Andreis, *Storia della città di Traù*, ed. Marco Perojević, Split, 1908, p. 306: "fra li suoi [of the church of S. Giovanni Battista] altari riguardevole più d'ogni altro è il fabbricato della famiglia Cippica, in cui s'adora un Cristo deposto di croce, così ben lavorato in marmo, ch'esige necessariamente la riverenza e la devozione: il fregiano bellissime figure di mezzo rilievo, che appassionate più dall'affetto che dalla punta dello scalpello, muovono un pietoso dolore della divina passione." For the dating of the manuscript to 1673 to 1676 see pp. xixf. of the introduction by Marco Perojević. In the late 1930s the 15th-century tomb slab of Pietro Cippico was still visible in the church: Ivo

Delalle, *Trogir. Vodić po njegovoj historiji umjetnosti i životv*, Split, n.d., p. 72.

35. Cvito Fisković, "Tri anđela Nikole Firentinca," *Napredak. Hrvatske narodni kalendar* (Sarajevo), xxx, 1941 (1940), p. 40.

36. Both *Genii* of this frieze were first attributed to Niccolò by Adolfo Venturi, "La scultura dalmata nel xv secolo," *L'arte*, xi, 1908, p. 119, and *idem, Storia*, vi, 1908, pp. 444ff. He rightly observed that the *Genii* must have been executed soon after Niccolò's arrival in Trogir, since the rest of the portal betrays the late Gothic architectural style of Aleši. Fisković, *op. cit.*, JAZU. Inst. za likovne umjetnosti. *Bulletin*, 1959, p. 26, attributed the twisting *Genius* to Niccolò, and the frontal one to an assistant. However, I would interpret the difference between the two *Genii* as one of composition—not style or quality.

37. Cvito Fisković, "Tri šibenska reljefa Nikole Firentinca," *Peristil*, iii, 1960, pp. 37ff. Fisković, *ibid.*, pp. 39f., attributed the *Angel* on the eastern side of the altar (right) to an assistant and the one on the western side (left) to Niccolò himself, reversing an earlier opinion (*idem*, "Bogorodica sa djetetom Nikole Firentinca u Orebićima," *Peristil*, ii, 1957, p. 171, n. 1) according to which both *Angels* were products of Niccolò's shop. I am in agreement concerning the differences between the two *Angels* but think that neither one is good enough to warrant attribution to Niccolò. Fisković, *op. cit.*, *Peristil*, 1960, p. 41, dated the figures to the last years of the 15th century.

38. The statue measures 66.8 cm. in height (including the head and halo), ca. 23 cm. in width, and ca. 15 cm. in depth. In addition to the loss of the original head and neck, there is a serious crack through the entire depth of the left side of the base. The lower left leg and foot are badly damaged. The toes of the right foot are missing, and the left hand has been patched with concrete. The scroll and knot of the mantle are chipped. Otherwise the surface is intact but badly worn. There is no inscription on the scroll.

39. The inscription in the frieze reads: "CONSSECRATVM MD · XXX · I · DIE · XII · NOVEMBRIS." The inscription in the arch of the lunette reads: "TEMPORE · R MI · DNI · IO · LVCII · EPI · SIBN · NEC · NON · PLEBANI · MARTINI · SAINI." (Giovanni Lucio was bishop of Šibenik from 1528 to 1557.)

40. See Appendix, p. 88. Since, at the time of the creation of the statue, the church was dedicated to the Trinity (P. Kolendić, "Stube na crkvi sv. Ivana u Šibeniku," *Starinar* [Belgrade], series 3, i, 1923, p. 65.) the statue is not likely to have occupied the center of an

earlier lunette above the main portal (though it might have been included in a group of three figures). The subject of the statue would have been most appropriate to the Confraternity of S. Giovanni di Monte which had its seat in the church and for which Giovanni Pribislavlich had already carved two external reliefs with the Baptist. (*Ibid.*, pp. 66f.) From the fact that the statue of the *Baptist* is made of the local rough gray limestone, widely used in Šibenik for construction, we may deduce that the figure was intended to be installed out-of-doors: sculptures destined for the interior of churches in Dalmatia are generally of Brać limestone or even marble. Indeed, its small scale would have made it a suitable embellishment for the balustrade of the external staircase constructed for the Confraternity of S. Giovanni di Monte.

41. Fisković, *op. cit.*, JAZU. Inst. za likovne umjetnosti. *Bulletin*, 1959, pp. 21ff., 24ff., made evident the superiority of the lion with the ram's head which he claimed as an autograph work by Niccolò di Giovanni, in contradistinction to its mate by an assistant. He effectively refuted the attribution of the two lions to Giovanni Dalmata advanced by Kruno Prijatelj, "Prinosi za monografiju o Ivanu Duknoviću," Dubrovnik. Historijski institut jugoslavenske akademije znanosti i umjetnosti. *Anali* (Dubrovnik), iv-v, 1956, pp. 308ff., and *idem, Ivan Duknović*, Zagreb, 1957, pp. 12f. Prijatelj's attribution was also rejected by Ljubo Karaman, "Razgovori o nekim problemima domaće historije, arheologije i historije umjetnosti," Dubrovnik. Historijski institut jugoslavenske akademije znanosti i umjetnosti. *Anali*, vi-vii, 1959, pp. 64ff., and Jolán Balogh, "Ioannes Duknovich de Tragurio," *Acta historiae artium*, vii, 1960, p. 58.

42. Ljubo Karaman, *Umjetnost u Dalmaciji xv. i xvi. vijek*, Zagreb, 1933, p. 91.

43. This statue is presumably identical with the statue of *Christ* finished in 1494. See Appendix, p. 85.

44. The pose of this *putto* derives from that of one of the *putti* in relief, now in the Museo Archeologico, Venice, which comes from the Neo-Attic "Throne of Saturn." The two reliefs of the "Throne of Saturn" in the Museo Archeologico are known to have arrived in Venice from Ravenna by 1335. In 1532 Jacopo Sansovino was ordered to remove them from beneath the windows of an arcade which led from Piazza S. Marco to the Frezzaria and install them in the Libreria. They were taken to S. Maria dei Miracoli instead where they remained until their removal to the museum in 1811. (See Giuseppe Valentinelli, *Marmi scolpiti del Museo Archeologico della Marciana di Venezia*, Prato, 1866, pp. 124ff., nos. 193, 199.) The influence of these reliefs, recognizable in

several of the *putti* of the frieze of the Baptistry at Trogir and in a *putto* of its baptismal font, is generally taken as a sign of Niccolò's intervention there.

45. For the iconography of the Orsini Chapel see Ivo Delalle, "Biser dalmatinske renesanse, Kapela sv. Ivana Ursina u trogirskoj katedrali," *Selo i grad, almanah*, v, 1933, pp. 67ff., and Jan Białostocki, "The Door of Death: Survival of a Classical Motif in Sepulchral Art," *Jahrbuch der Hamburger Kunstsammlungen*, xviii, 1973, pp. 23f.

46. P. Kolendić, "Documenti o Andriji Alešiju u Trogiru," Belgrade. Univerzitet. Seminar za arbanašku filologiju. *Arkhiv za arbanašku starinu jezik i etnologiju*, ii, 1924, p. 75.

47. See Appendix, p. 85.

48. In the middle of the flattened and simplified rear face of the statue of *Christ* is a large square hole used for fastening the figure to the wall like the one at the back of the statue of *St. John the Evangelist* carved for the chapel by Giovanni Dalmata. For an illustration of the rear of the latter statue see Cvito Fisković, "Duknovićev kip apostola Ivana u Trogiru," *Peristil*, xiv–xv, 1971–72, p. 125, fig. 5.

49. Cvito Fisković, "Zabat tabernakula Nikole Firentinca u Šibeniku," Matica srpska, Novi sad. Odeljenje za umetnost. *Zbornik za likovne umetnosti*, xii, 1976, p. 244, n. 13, recently suggested that the original group was removed because the recess in which the group stood or was intended to stand was changed from a semicircular niche to the three-sided alcove with splayed lateral walls which now exists. As evidence of the existence of an original semicircular niche, Fisković referred to the discovery by Bryan Ward-Perkins of life-size drawings of plans and elevations of the chapel incised on the original flag-stone roof over the north aisle of the Cathedral at Trogir. Fisković's report, however, is erroneous: the plan of the chapel's rear wall, which, as Ward-Perkins shows, was made during the course of construction of the chapel, does not possess a semicircular niche, but rather a trapezoidal recess like the niche found there today. See Bryan Ward-Perkins and Sheila Gibson, "The Incised Architectural Drawings of Trogir Cathedral," *Antiquaries Journal*, lvii, in press.

50. Compare, for example, the iconography of Giambattista and Lorenzo Bregno's Cappella del Santissimo Sacramento, Duomo, Treviso, with its *Resurrected Christ* of 1506–8 in the central niche at the head of the chapel, flanked by two angels and two apostles.

III The Life and Art of Niccolò di Giovanni Fiorentino

O UR ATTRIBUTION to Niccolò di Giovanni of six Venetian monuments dated between 1457 and 1467 completes for the first time the biography of this sculptor with an account of his activity prior to his arrival in Dalmatia. That he came from Florence is strongly suggested by the epithet "fiorentino" so frequently recorded in the documents. On the basis of the style of his Dalmatian works it is generally assumed that Niccolò was trained in Padua in Donatello's workshop. He is often identified with the Niccolò Coccari da Firenze employed by Donatello on the carving of the stonework of the tabernacle which housed the figures of the High Altar of the Santo.[1] In addition to the facts that no patronymic is recorded for Niccolò Coccari and that Niccolò di Giovanni is never called Coccari, there is good reason to think that Coccari and Niccolò di Giovanni are not the same person. At his first appearance in the Santo documents Coccari already was a master and had formed a partnership with Meo and Pipo da Firenze. The work for which he alone was paid comprised the most banal tasks of his trade: on February 12, 1449, Coccari was credited for eight marble columns; on February 22, 1449, he was paid for having worked on "the stones that go at the back of the altar" and for having carved some marble cornices. For the latter work he was paid the modest wage of 20 soldi per day—the same wage earned by Meo and Pipo and by Bartolomeo Bon when he received his first independent commission. Thus by 1448 Coccari was a trained and qualified master whose capabilities must have been very limited and whose specialty was carving architectural details.

69

On the other hand, all indices derived from his Venetian works suggest that in 1457 Niccolò di Giovanni was young and that his rise was meteoric. It is conceivable that as a *discepolo* or *garzone* Donatello might have set him to carving cornices, but by the time he had become a master his extraordinary talent would surely have been manifest.

Nevertheless, it is possible that Niccolò was trained in Donatello's Paduan workshop. He was artistically formed by the experience of modeling and no place more easily than in Donatello's shop, where major works for casting in bronze were modeled without interruption in the decade of the 1440s, could he have been trained in that technique. Niccolò's work demonstrates familiarity with the Paduan sculptures of Donatello, with the *Gattamelata* cast in 1447 and installed in September 1453 and the High Altar of the Santo of 1446–50. The portrait of *Gattamelata* determined the portrayal of Francesco Foscari and Vittore Capello. A winged head located on the breast in the armor of the *Gattamelata* reappears in the figure of *Capello*, and the cherub's head which fastens the cloak of the *Madonna* in the Santo altar recurs frequently in works by Niccolò.[2] The partly opened door, used first in a Renaissance funerary context in the Brancacci Tomb in Naples, appears also in the base of the *Gattamelata* (though here the door is nearly shut); it is presumably the latter example which inspired its adaptation in the Orsini Chapel where torch-bearing *putti* pass through the doors as though into the real space of the chapel. The disposition of *Virtues* around the *Effigy of Foscari* and the exaggerated movement of the figures reflect innovations of the High Altar of the Santo. The face of *Prudence* is related to the *Madonna*'s face. The mourning woman in the *Lamentation* from the Sobota Tomb recalls a comparable figure in the *Lamentation* from the Santo altar. At Padua Niccolò learned to know the landscapes and drapery style of Mantegna; even after his move to Venice, Niccolò remained in contact with the painter, drawing on a contemporary work by Mantegna for the figure of *Christ* in the Foscari Tomb. But Niccolò was also familiar with Donatello's Florentine works. Indeed, his idiosyncratic drapery style is closer to Donatello's sculpture of the 1430s—the *Cantoria* and stucco *Evangelists*, and prophets from the bronze doors, of the Old Sacristy in S. Lorenzo—and to works dependent on them, such as Agostino di Duccio's Altar of S. Gimignano for the Cathedral at Modena of 1442, than it is to Donatello's sculptures for the Santo altar. The head of *St. Stephen* from the stucco reliefs of the Old Sacristy strikingly resembles the physiognomy of the left-hand *Foscari Warrior*. The cherub in the left sacristy spandrel above *SS. Cosmas* and *Damian* is so similar to the head of Christ's angelic companion in the Foscari Tomb that it might have been executed by Niccolò himself. We may therefore surmise that Niccolò began his training under Donatello before the latter's move to Padua and that Donatello's presence there caused Niccolò to follow. That Niccolò renewed acquaintance with Donatello's work toward the end of his career is proved by his relief of *Christ Carried to the Tomb* in S. Maria di Valverde (Frontispiece), indebted for its intensity of feeling as well as for numerous motifs to the reliefs of Donatello's pulpits in S. Lorenzo. From Dona-tello's *Crucifixion* Niccolò borrowed the figures of John the Evangelist and the man imme-diately behind him and the woman with lowered arms rushing forward on the left. From Donatello's *Lamentation* he took the frantic mourner with upraised arms. The flanking fig-ure leaning on a staff in front of the relief space corresponds to a figure from Donatello's *Entombment*, which, doubtless, also inspired the low point of sight. The half-length figure in the foreground visible on the right of Niccolò's relief can be traced to several panels of the pulpits. In Donatello's *Lamentation* such a figure similarly placed at the border of the com-position seems to rise out of the ground. From the last three scenes of the Passion cycle of the pulpits comes the arched architectural backdrop—so extraordinary in a scene of *Christ Carried to the Tomb*—running across the entire width of the relief parallel to the plane of its background at a short distance from the foreground. Indeed, it would be no exaggeration to say that Niccolò di Giovanni remained Donatello's most faithful follower. Perhaps he would not have done so had he continued to work in Venice or Florence where he might have responded to the inventions of other first-rate artists. But in Dalmatia he was supreme and can have found little stimulus outside his memories.

Niccolò's first work in Venice, datable soon after the doge's death on November 1, 1457, was the Tomb of Francesco Foscari. Why was a young and presumably little known Florentine awarded such a prestigious commission? Possibly because Bartolomeo Bon, the only other sculptor active in Venice at the time and capable of producing a work of com-parable quality, was engaged in the far vaster undertaking of the construction and decora-tion of the Arco Foscari. Moreover, the fact that Bartolomeo was the favored architect and sculptor of that government which had just deposed the doge may have militated against his employment by the doge's heirs. Nor was the choice of a Florentine without precedent: the tomb of Foscari's precedessor, Tomaso Mocenigo, had been entrusted to the Florentine Pietro Lamberti, and to Giovanni di Martino da Fiesole. Niccolò's employment on the Arco Foscari and the portal of the Madonna dell'Orto cannot be dated with exactitude or cer-tainty, but probably it followed shortly upon the death of Bartolomeo Bon, mentioned as alive for the last time on August 8, 1464. Most of the work on the Tomb of Orsato Giustini-ani, who died on July 11, 1464, must postdate April 1466 when the executors of Giustiniani's testament, under legal pressure, announced their intention of disbursing the money which Giustiniani had designated for his tomb. Probably it was not yet complete when Niccolò emigrated to Dalmatia, for parts of it seem not even to have been supervised by him. The Tomb of Vittore Capello cannot have been commenced before early April 1467 when news of his death reached Venice. Its execution probably continued into 1468. It is not possible to say whether the relief of *St. Jerome* was made in Venice or Dalmatia—a work of this small size could easily have been exported, as was the stone, in any case. Nevertheless, a *terminus ante quem* for it, the one identical to it in Dubrovnik, or a hypothetical prototype, is provided by Aleši's relief of *St. Jerome* in Liverpool datable to the tenure of Count Alvise Lando between 1470 and 1472.

On December 19, 1467, Niccolò di Giovanni makes his first appearance in the documents of Trogir: on that day he constituted Coriolano Cippico his representative for the signing of a joint contract with Andrea Aleši for the construction of the Chapel of Blessed Giovanni Orsini in the Cathedral of Trogir. At the immense cost of 2,300 ducats, this contract envisaged one of the most elaborate schemes of architectural and sculptural interior decoration in the fifteenth century. It is therefore understandable that, in order to undertake the project, Niccolò abandoned the assured position I suggest he occupied at Venice. At the same time, the administrators of the Cathedral would not have entrusted such an important commission to a sculptor who had not already distinguished himself. Naturally they looked to Venice, the political and artistic focus of Dalmatia, most of which had come under Venetian rule in 1420, just as the procurators of the Cathedral of Šibenik had done when seeking a *protomaestro* for their church several decades earlier. Perhaps Coriolano Cippico, friend of the Venetian historian Marc'Antonio Sabellico and subsequently commander of a galley under Pietro Mocenigo in the wars against the Turks, was instrumental in bringing Niccolò to Trogir. Niccolò's appearance in Trogir in mid-December 1467, however, evidently was no more than a short visit made for the purpose of negotiating a contract with the *Opera del Duomo*, for on January 4, 1468, at the actual writing of the contract, Niccolò was no longer present and his name does not reappear in the documents of Trogir until April 26, 1468. One may hypothesize that Niccolò returned to Venice in order to finish the Tomb of Vittore Capello. Niccolò's own activity in Dalmatia was preceded by that of a sculptor possibly trained and certainly influenced by him: the style of the Altarpiece of St. Jerome, Christ, and John the Baptist in the cemetery church of St. Cyprian in Praznice on the island of Brač, inscribed with the date of 1467, represents a provincial interpretation of Niccolò's art.[3] Niccolò's first works in Trogir are probably the *putti* he contributed to the frieze in Aleši's Baptistry. Above its door, the internal wall bears the date of 1467.[4] This date is generally thought to refer to the completion of the building and thus is used to prove that Niccolò was already settled in Trogir by 1467.[5] However, there is no inherent reason why the date should refer to the completion of the work. Indeed, if, as was customary and as was certainly the case with the *putti* in the frieze,[6] the inscription was carved before the installation of the block—an integral member of the wall—then a major portion of the architectural work on the Baptistry and all its decoration still remained to be executed, and only with exceptional foresight could the carver have known the date of the completion of the work. It seems far more probable that the date refers to the foundation of the Baptistry and that work on it continued at least into 1468.

Progress on the Orsini Chapel was fitful. On November 24, 1475, Niccolò and Aleši complained for the second time that they had not been paid and that the site on which the foundations were to be sunk had not been cleared. In 1477 a house in the possession of the Cathedral was exchanged for certain places surrounding the site of the new chapel. Coriolano Cippico acted as intermediary. The first statue—that of *St. John the Evangelist*—was delivered only in 1482. In 1487 Niccolò was paid for the statues of *Christ*, the *Virgin*, and *St. Peter*. In 1488 Niccolò finished the statue of *St. John the Baptist*, and in 1489 he delivered four more statues. A second statue of *Christ* was completed in 1494 for the same price as the other five immediately preceding ones. This is probably the *Resurrected Christ*. Meanwhile, in the contract of July 1, 1477, in which he was named *protomaestro* of the Cathedral of Šibenik, Niccolò was granted permission to go to Trogir for two or three days at a time when business demanded. From the renewal of his contract at Šibenik of February 12, 1497, we learn that Niccolò was still under obligation to the *Opera del Duomo* of Trogir for the "work begun a long time ago in said church and for finishing the figures which he is obligated to make for that work." The administrators of the Cathedral of Šibenik therefore granted him permission to carve a stone figure, either alone or together with his son who was being trained by him, and to execute that work either at the quarry or in the stone workshop. At Niccolò's death in 1505 all the statues still had not been furnished. A second statue of *John the Evangelist* is inscribed "IOANNIS DAMATAE F." and is probably the one recorded as finished by "Magistro Joanne lapicida" in 1508. In 1559 four final statues were supplied by Alessandro Vittoria but Beato Giovanni Orsini was not buried in the chapel until 1681.

On November 30, 1472, a final quittance was given for payment for minor work of restoration executed jointly by Aleši and Niccolò on the Campanile of St. Domnius at Split. By October 20, 1473, work for S. Maria degli Agostiniani on S. Niccolò delle Tremiti, again undertaken jointly by Aleši and Niccolò, had been completed. In addition to the facade, they had erected there an elaborate portal consisting of two rows of superposed niches containing statues, including a *St. Paul*, flanking two reliefs. The lower one, framed in a lunette, once portrayed *St. Augustine Consigning His Rule* to kneeling monks. The upper one depicts the *Assumption of the Virgin* who hands her girdle to St. Thomas. At the top, two *putti*, not envisaged in the original contract, flank a candelabrum.[7] In the autumn of 1473 Aleši and Niccolò had not yet received the final 76 ducats out of a salary of 700 ducats. They sued to have it but were not satisfied till 1480 after endless legal complications.

On October 10, 1473, Giorgio da Sebenico died, leaving vacant the post of *protomaestro* of the Cathedral of St. James at Šibenik.[8] On October 16, 1475, Niccolò, already called *protomaestro* of St. James, makes his first appearance in the documents of Šibenik. From this time forward no commissions were accepted jointly with Aleši, and although on November 24, 1475, the two appear as *compagni* for legal purposes in connection with the Orsini Chapel, by that date their partnership had probably been dissolved. Despite his continued supervision of the Orsini Chapel, from this time forth the focus of Niccolò's activity was Šibenik. On October 16, 1475, Niccolò was commissioned by the Confraternity of S. Giovanni di Monte to erect the balustrade of the stairs previously constructed by Giovanni Pribislavlich along an exterior flank of the church of St. John the Baptist. Niccolò received his salary as architect of the Cathedral in October 1476 and February 1477, yet the contract in which he was formally appointed *protomaestro* for the following ten years (to be counted from the previous May 1) dates only from July 1, 1477. On February 12, 1497, his contract was renewed. On January 25, 1499, Niccolò was commissioned to carve the balustrades of the *cantorie* and of the choir at the east end of the Cathedral.

Niccolò, present in Zadar but designated "inhabitant of Trogir," was commissioned on October 24, 1485, by Deodato Venier, abbot of the monastery of S. Crisogono at Zadar, to carve two windows with "their proportionate embellishments and figures" for the monastery's courtyard.

By January 10, 1502, Niccolò had received the citizenship of Šibenik. On that day he was appointed *protomaestro* of the church of S. Maria di Valverde at Šibenik for the following five years in order to supervise construction of the church. Niccolò received his last wages from the church on May 31, 1505. Apparently he died sometime during the second half of 1505, for on January 1, 1506—a year before the termination of Niccolò's contract—the *Operai* of the church made an independent agreement with another master for the acquisition of a large quantity of material. Immured in the second story of the courtyard of the church is the relief by Niccolò of *Christ Carried to the Tomb* which Niccolò never lived to finish but which, for its sublimity of conception and force of execution, rivals Donatello.[9]

Two undocumented works not yet considered can be attributed to Niccolò's own hand. One is the badly worn Tomb slab of Jacopo Torlono, bishop of Trogir from 1452 until his death in 1483, immured immediately to the left of the entrance to the Orsini Chapel in the Cathedral of Trogir.[10] Commissioned by his brother, Ermolao, the tomb slab of the bishop originally covered Torlono's grave in the pavement of the chapel whose foundation he oversaw.[11] An under life-size free-standing statue of *St. Sebastian* in the Muzej grada of Trogir (Fig. 98) is surely also autograph. The figure comes from the main altar of the tiny church of St. Sebastian at Trogir. Coats of arms on the facade and bell tower of the church date its construction to the tenure as count of Troilo Malipiero (1477–80) and Niccolò Pisani (1480–82) and to the episcopacy of Jacopo Torlono. It is likely that the statue is coeval with the construction of the church.[12]

Whether most of the myriad sculptures in Dalmatia associated with Niccolò Fiorentino were actually executed in his shop or merely reflect his influence we do not know. Nevertheless, their range and number indicate that the effect of Niccolò's art was pervasive and long-lasting. Indeed, it is no exaggeration to say that it produced a revolution in Dalmatian sculpture which met with no resistance for over half a century. Sculptures found in centers in which Niccolò is known to have been active are generally closer in style to the master's own works and higher in quality than those found in provincial churches and may, indeed, be products of his shop. At Trogir such works include the small triptych with the *Madonna and Child* flanked by *SS. Jerome and Ladislas*[13] and the pair of brackets with two addorsed *putti* supporting the architrave of Radovan's portal in the Cathedral;[14] in St. Dominic the triptych with *Beato Giovanni Orsini* and *SS. Jerome* and *Lawrence*;[15] on the facade of the bell-tower of St. Sebastian the two pairs of *putti* holding Malipiero and Torlono arms and the statues of *St. Sebastian* and *Christ*;[16] in the cemetery the medallion with the bust of *God the Father* which originally occupied the center of the vault of the Orsini Chapel[17] and two mutilated free-standing *Angels* with bowls which originally flanked the group of the *Ascending Christ*;[18] in the Muzej grada the relief of an *Angel* with a torch[19] and fragments of two *putti* with a vase and garlands, possibly from the lunette of an altar.[20] The bust-length statue of *St. Peter* over the portal of the homonymous church at Trogir and the miniature figure of the seated *St. Nicholas* on the exterior of Trogir's St. Nicholas[21] are more distant in quality and style and probably represent late reflections of Niccolò's art. At Šibenik, in addition to the statuary and reliefs which ornament the Cathedral, the marble gable of an altarpiece or tabernacle carved in high relief with *putti*, cornucopias, vase, and crown of thorns,[22] and the relief of two *putti* with a coat of arms, both in museums of the city, may be counted among the products of Niccolò's shop.[23] At Zadar the reliefs beneath the windows of the Casa dei Ghirardini and the Casa dei Pasini (of which only a fragment is preserved in the Narodni Muzej),[24] the lunette with two *putti* holding a shield with the Da Ponte arms also in the Narodni Muzej,[25] and the plaque with two *putti* and the Detrico coat of arms in the Chapel of the Holy Cross in St. Francis[26] betray the style, if not the hand, of Niccolò Fiorentino. At Split reflections of his art have been identified in the damaged *Pietà* from the lunette of the portal of St. Eufemia, now in the museum of the city,[27] and in the relief of the *Madonna and Child* of 1503 on the city gate tentatively attributed to Niccolò's pupil, Marin Vladić of Brač.[28] The small statue of *St. Stephen* in the cemetery church of the same name at Sumpetar Poljički was carved by a sculptor influenced, if not supervised, by Niccolò.[29] Farther afield, the influence of Niccolò is recognizable in the statue of *St. Peter* from the facade of the homonymous church at Vrboske (island of Hvar)[30] and at Hvar in the lunette with the *Madonna and Child and Two Angels* over the portal of St. Francis[31] and in the lunette with the *Annunciation* over the portal of the church of the SS. Annunziata.[32] The art of Niccolò Fiorentino affected the portrayal of the *Madonna and Child* in the relief on a lateral altar in the church of the Madonna dell'Angelo at Orebić.[33]

On the island of Brač his influence is apparent in the altarpiece with the reliefs of *St. George and the Dragon*, *Christ as Man of Sorrows*, and the *Madonna and Child* in St. George at Straževnik[34] and in the altar with the *Madonna and Child* flanked by *SS. John the Baptist* and *Peter* in the cemetery church of St. Mary, Gorni Humac.[35]

Niccolò's career spanned nearly half a century during which his style naturally underwent a change. In spite of the fact that the boundaries of Niccolò's autograph works are not invariably clear—one cannot always be certain whether the inferior quality of many of Niccolò's works, especially those in the Orsini Chapel, are due to the participation of assistants or to the artist's lassitude as he grew older—it is possible to discover, from comparison with Dalmatian works whose authenticity is indisputable, the nature of this change.

The *Coronation of the Virgin* in the lunette beneath the vault of the Orsini Chapel (Fig. 99) is undated, but from the building history of the chapel we can infer for it a date not earlier than the late 1470s. A comparison with *Fortitude* from the Foscari Tomb (Fig. 17) makes evident the linear and methodic treatment of the Virgin's drapery. Broken and irregular folds are replaced by long, parallel strips whose regular contours conform to catenary curves. Edges of folds are harder and more precise because their tops are smoother and their sides more consistently faceted. Areas between folds are almost invariably smooth and their borders—generally teardrop in shape—are more completely and explicitly defined by grooves. Grooves are straighter, often parallel, and furrow a more planar surface. Drapery takes less account of the volume and anatomy of the body underneath. If the pattern made by folds is sometimes no more abstract than in the early works, it always is more obvious.

A comparison of the Virgin with the *Annunciate Virgin* of the Foscari Tomb (Fig. 30) shows how much more flatly and schematically a later work treats the same gesture and to what extent its decorative and abstract qualities have been accentuated at the expense of naturalistic detail. The differentiated folds of the *Annunciate*'s sleeves are replaced by a dense network of similar grooves. All anatomical detail has been banished from the even surface of the hands, turned forward in order to produce a calligraphic silhouette. The unusual motif common to both, of the veil doubled back over one ear, occasions in the early work independent, superimposed strata deeply undercut. In the later work the veil is wound tightly around the head so that head, hair, and veil are consolidated into a sphere.

The statue of *St. Michael* crowning the north transept of the Cathedral of Šibenik (Fig. 97) postdates the *Foscari Warrior* (Fig. 11) by at least fifteen years and probably a good deal more. The same stance and canon of proportions have been employed for both, yet subtle adjustments in the disposition of *St. Michael*'s limbs have transformed the meandering design of the *Foscari Warrior* into a tectonic and precisely balanced composition. Contours are less broken, and the borders provided by the armor delineate regular geometric shapes.

Folds, reduced in number, are graphically defined as long and regular projecting strips. Between these two extremes, the *Moro Warrior* from the Arco Foscari (Fig. 38) represents an intermediate stage.

The same imposition of a tectonic grid on a uniform and planar surface, the same substitution of a graphic for a plastic definition of form, the same commingling of geometric shapes and calligraphic lines are revealed by a comparison of the face of the *Foscari Warrior* (Fig. 13) with the head of *St. Sebastian* in the Muzej grada at Trogir (Fig. 98). What is essentially the physiognomy of the *Foscari Warrior* has been made more regular in the *St. Sebastian*. Its mass has been compressed into a cube, the uniformity of whose front face is preserved by eyes that barely recede within their sockets and a nose that hardly projects. Strenuously modeled surfaces are smoothed. Incised boundaries circumscribe with greater clarity and exactitude the lineaments of the face. The hair is still composed of thick wooly tufts, but the tufts have merged to give the head a smoothly rounded surface. The ears have acquired a largely ornamental value.

The trajectory of Niccolò's development is not an uncommon one for artists whose careers span so many years. Indeed, it recapitulates in the space of a single lifetime a pattern of artistic development seen at diverse intervals throughout the history of art. One need only think of the evolution of early to late archaic Greek art, early to high Romanesque sculpture, early to late Quattrocento Florentine painting, to see how fundamental is the evolution from a plastic, naturalistic art expressive of youthful curiosity and enthusiasm to a flat and ornamental art predicated on a technical mastery achieved through long experience. The repetitiveness and schematism of a highly developed art betray a flagging of creative energies as common to civilizations as to individuals. Yet in spite of this, Niccolò's concern for dramatic values and the inventiveness with which he embodied them characterize even his later works as emanations of genius. In his *Coronation of the Virgin* (Fig. 100) Niccolò seated his figures at opposite ends of an exceptionally broad throne.[36] The figures strain to reach each other: so great is the effort of Christ's movement that his cloak flies out behind him in response to it. Thus the convergence of the figures has the force and ineluctability of magnetic attraction. At the same time, Christ is about to set on Mary's head a colossal crown in expectation of whose weight she is already bowed, accepting humbly the burdens to which her exaltation calls her. Not the joyous celebration of the Virgin's sanctity has Niccolò chosen to present but her passive resignation, as though the end were a new beginning to the cycle of redemption.

NOTES

1. This identification was first made by Adolfo Venturi, "La scultura dalmata nel xv secolo," *L'arte*, xi, 1908, pp. 113f., and corrected by Erice Rigoni, "Il soggiorno in Padova di Nicolò Baroncelli," Padua. Accademia di scienze lettere ed arti. *Atti e memorie*, n.s. xliii, 1926–27, pp. 227ff. For the documents concerning Niccolò Coccari see Antonio Sartori, "Documenti riguardanti Donatello e il suo altare di Padova," *Il Santo*, i, 1961, pp. 76, 77, 78, 79. Cvito Fisković, *Zadarski sredovječni majstori*, Split, 1959, p. 58, reported work in progress in 1450 on the house in Via S. Michele in Zadar of a certain Nicola Cocari. A document of Zadar of 1509 informs us that he had died: Fisković, "Aleši, Firentinac i Duknović u Trogiru," Jugoslavenska akademija znanosti i umjetnosti. Institut za likovne umjetnosti. *Bulletin* (Zagreb), vii, 1959, p. 42, n. 21. There is no particular reason for identifying this Nicola Cocari with Donatello's assistant, and even less with Niccolò di Giovanni Fiorentino.

2. Cvito Fisković, "Bogorodica sa djetetom Nikole Firentinca u Orebićima," *Peristil*, ii, 1957, p. 174.

3. The inscription reads: "м̃ · CCCC · LXVII · TĒPORE · DÑI · PB̄RI · MARINI · ś · IHERONIMI." This relief was first viewed as providing a *terminus ante quem* for the influence of Niccolò's art in Dalmatia by Ljubo Karaman, *Umjetnost u Dalmaciji xv. i xvi. vijek*, Zagreb, 1933, p. 72, n. 19. For the relief see Kruno Prijatelj, "Novi vijek," *BBački zbornik* (Supetar), iv, 1960, pp. 164ff. Prijatelj, *ibid.*, p. 164, thought that Niccolò's arrival in Dalmatia actually predated the relief.

4. The inscription reads: "IACOBO · TORLONO · PONTIFICE · / CAROLO · CAPELLO · PRAETORE · / ANDREAS · ALEXIVS · / DVRRACHINVS · OPIFEX · MCCCCLXVII."

5. Fisković, *op. cit.*, JAZU. Inst. za likovne umjetnosti. *Bulletin*, 1959, pp. 23f.; Davor Domančić, "Reljef Nikole Firentinca u Hvaru," *Prilozi povijesti umjetnosti u Dalmaciji* (Split), xii, 1960, p. 177; Rózsa Feuer-Tóth, "Le rôle de la Dalmatie dans l'expansion de la renaissance florentine en Hongrie," *Évolution générale et développements régionaux en histoire de l'art* (Actes du xxiie Congrès International d'Histoire de l'Art, Budapest, 1969), Budapest, 1972, i, p. 626.

On the other hand, Fisković, "Radovi Nikole Firentinca u Zadru," *Peristil*, iv, 1961, p. 71, dated Niccolò's arrival in Trogir to ca. 1457 on the basis of an inscription found—no longer in its original position—in the courtyard of Cippico's new palace. The inscription reads: "CORIOLANVS · CIPCVS · / P · F · HEC · STATVENDA · / CVRAVIT · SIBI · ET · CVI · DEVS · / DEDERIT · MCCCCLVII." Fisković unjustifiably applied the date of Coriolano's attention to the construction of "these things" to Niccolò's work on the lateral portal of the palace.

6. Folnesics, *Jahrb. Zentralkomm.*, 1914, p. 132.

7. Bruno Molajoli, "Monumenti e opere d'arte nell'isola di S. Nicola delle Tremiti," *Iapigia* (Bari), vi, 1935, pp. 405ff., whose description is more accurate than that of Fisković, *op. cit.*, *Peristil*, 1961, p. 73, n. 25a. (I am grateful to Prof. Ulrich Middeldorf for the first of these references.)

8. Giorgio was mentioned alive for the last time in a document of May 20, 1473. (Petar Kolendić, "Slikar Juraj Ćulinović u Šibeniku," *Vjesnik za arheologiju i historiju dalmatinsku* [Sarajevo/Split], xliii, 1920, p. 126, n. 2.) He was dead by May 25, 1474. (*Ibid.*, p. 135, no. 32.) The anniversary of his death was celebrated on October 10. (Frey-Molè, p. 162, doc. 153.)

9. Frey-Molè, pp. 41f.; Folnesics, *Jahrb. Zentralkomm.*, 1914, p. 169; Wolfgang Wolters, "Due capolavori della cerchia di Donatello a Trogir e a Šibenik," *Antichità viva*, vii, no. 1, January–February 1968, pp. 15ff., esp. p. 24, n. 15.

10. Venturi, *op. cit.*, *L'arte*, 1908, p. 117.

11. Vincenzo de Celio-Cega, *La chiesa di Traù*, Split, 1855, p. 27, no. XI.

12. Cvito Fisković, "Firentinčev Sebastijan u Trogiru," *Zbornik za umetnostno zgodovino* (Ljubljana), n.s. v–vi, 1959, pp. 369, 375f., 378ff.

13. Venturi, *op. cit.*, *L'arte*, 1908, pp. 113, 114, 117.

14. *Ibid.*, p. 119.

15. *Ibid.*, pp. 120f.

16. Fisković, *op. cit.*, *Zbornik za umetnostno zgodovino*, 1959, pp. 378ff.

17. Cvito Fisković, "Ignacije Macanović i njegov krug," *Prilozi povijesti umjetnosti u Dalmaciji*, ix, 1955, p. 258.

18. *Idem*, "Tri anđela Nikole Firentinca," *Napredak. Hrvatske narodni kalendar* (Sarajevo), xxx, 1941 (1940), pp. 37ff.

19. *Ibid.*, pp. 39f.

20. Fisković, *op. cit.*, *Zbornik za umetnostno zgodovino*, 1959, pp. 377f.

21. *Idem*, "Neobjavljeni Firentinčev reljef u Trogiru," *Slobodna Dalmacija* (Split), August 14, 1976, p. 7.

22. Cvito Fisković, "Zabat tabernakula Nikole Firentinca u Šibeniku," Matica srpska, Novi sad. Odeljenje za umetnost. *Zbornik za likovne umetnosti*, xii, 1976, pp. 239ff.

23. *Idem*, "Tri šibenska reljefa Nikole Firentinca," *Peristil*, iii, 1960, p. 41.

24. *Idem*, *op. cit.*, *Peristil*, 1961, pp. 61ff.

25. *Ibid.*, pp. 63ff.

26. *Ibid.*, pp. 65f.

27. Duško Kečkemet, "Renesansna klesarsko-kiparska djela u Splitu," *Prilozi povijesti umjetnosti u Dalmaciji*, vii, 1953, p. 80.

28. Ksenija Cicarelli, "Reljef Firentičeve škole u Splitu," *Prilozi povijesti umjetnosti u Dalmaciji*, vii, 1953, pp. 29ff.

29. Vladimir Gvozdanović, "Prilog radionici Nikole Firentinca i Andrije Alešija," *Peristil*, x–xi, 1967–68, pp. 62f.

30. *Ibid.*, pp. 59ff.

31. Davor Domančić, *op. cit.*, *Prilozi povijesti umjetnosti u Dalmaciji*, 1960, pp. 172ff.

32. *Ibid.*, p. 179.

33. Cvito Fisković, "Bogorodica sa djetetom Nikole Firentinca u Orebićima," *Peristil*, ii, 1957, pp. 172ff.

34. Kruno Prijatelj, *op. cit.*, *Brački zbornik*, 1960, pp. 167ff.

35. *Ibid.*, pp. 169f.

36. Dr. Marilyn Aronberg Lavin has suggested that the breadth and shape of the throne make of it a symbol of Ecclesia.

APPENDIX Digest of
Documents concerning
the Life and Works of
Niccolò di Giovanni Fiorentino

SOURCES OF PUBLISHED DOCUMENTS

Joso Felicinović, "Metajna," *Narodna Politika* (Zagreb), xii, no. 67, June 12, 1928, p. 2.

Cvito Fisković, *Opis trogirske katedrale iz xviii stoljeća*, Split, 1940.

Idem, "Aleši, Firentinac i Duknović u Trogiru," Jugoslavenska akademija znanosti i umjetnosti. Institut za likovne umjetnosti. *Bulletin* (Zagreb), vii, 1959, pp. 20-43.

Dagobert Frey, "Der Dom von Sebenico und sein Baumeister Giorgio Orsini," with an appendix of documents by Vojeslav Molè, *Jahrbuch des kunsthistorischen Institutes der k. k. Zentral-kommission für Denkmalpflege*, vii, 1913, pp. 1-169.

Petar Kolendić, "Stube na crkvi sv. Ivana u Šibeniku," *Starinar* (Belgrade), series 3, i, 1923, pp. 65-94.

Idem, "Documenti o Andriji Alešiju u Trogiru," Belgrade. Univerzitet. Seminar za arbanašku filologiju. *Arkhiv za arbanašku starinu jezik i etnologiju*, ii, 1924, pp. 70-78.

Idem, "Šibenska katedrala pre dolaska Orsinijeva (1430.-1441.)," *Narodna starina* (Zagreb), series 8, iii, no. 2, 1924, pp. 154-175.

Idem, "Aleši i Firentinac na Tremitima," Skopsko naučno drustvo. *Glasnik* (Skopje), i, 1925, pp. 205-214.

L. Kukuljević, "Aleksijev Andrija Dračanin," *Slovnik umjetnikah jugoslavenskih*, Zagreb, i, 1858, pp. 4–10.

Vincenzo Miagostovich, *I nobili e il clero di Sebenico nel 1449 per la fabbrica della Cattedrale*, Šibenik, 1910, Appendix II, pp. 61–64.

Giuseppe Praga, "Documenti intorno ad Andrea Alessi," *Rassegna marchigiana*, viii, 1929–30, pp. 1–26.

Kruno Prijatelj, "Boravak Nikole Firentinca u Zadru," *Prilozi povijesti umjetnosti u Dalmaciji* (Split), xiii, 1961, pp. 227–232.

With very few and insignificant exceptions the documents summarized below were published in entirety or in part in their original Latin or Italian. The rest occur as paraphrases in the texts in which they are reported. Summaries made from Latin and Italian documents are the author's own. Paraphrases in Serbo-Croatian were translated by Mr. Pierre Djokić.

CHAPEL OF BEATO GIOVANNI ORSINI, CATHEDRAL, TROGIR

December 19, 1467 Maestro Niccolò quondam Giovanni, stonemason, present in Trogir, constituted Coriolano Cippico his procurator for the purpose of making a contract jointly with Andrea Aleši, with the administrator of the cathedral church of S. Lorenzo in Trogir for the construction of a chapel in that church. (Kolendić, *Arkhiv*, 1924, p. 73, doc. vi.) January 4, 1468 Aleši and Niccolò Fiorentino, the latter represented by Cippico, made a contract with ser Nicolò quondam ser Cipriani, administrator, for the construction of the Chapel of Beato Giovanni. Drawings of the projected chapel had been made and were to be kept in a box in the chancellery of the commune. Aleši and Niccolò were to demolish the exterior wall of the Cathedral behind the altar of St. Ursula and there they were to erect two pilasters on a step. The pilasters were to measure 17 feet in height. Their front faces were to measure $1\frac{1}{2}$ feet in width and their lateral faces, 2 feet. They were to support a semicircular arch $1\frac{1}{2}$ feet in width on its front face and 2 feet in depth, with a diameter of about 10 feet. In the keystone (?: "straia") of the arch there was to lie a figure 3 feet high. Both faces of the arch were to be carved. Between the pilasters there were to be two pieces of a fretted balustrade about 3 feet high and two figures 3 feet high for each of the two corners within the church. On its exterior the chapel was to measure 24 feet long by 24 feet wide. Inside, the chapel was to measure 20 feet in length by 15 feet in width by 17 feet in height to the springing of the semicircular vault. The pavement of the chapel was to be made of squares of white and red Veronese stone, each about one foot square. The altar was to rest on two steps. Either it was to consist of a slab $4\frac{1}{2}$ by $2\frac{1}{2}$ feet with moldings, supported by four pedestals, as in the drawing, or else it was to be made like a box with two angels in half relief on the front face. The marble shrine of the saint which was then in the church was also to rest on the steps. It was to be carved on three sides with four scenes of miracles from the life of the saint while the fourth side was to be coffered. The cover of the shrine, to be made of stone from

Voluje, was to have moldings. The shrine was to be supported by four angels, each 4 feet high. Three figures, each 3 feet high, were to be placed on the altar in front of the shrine. The interior of the chapel was to be surrounded by a bench whose projecting lower face, $1\frac{1}{2}$ feet high, was to be carved like that of the Baptistry though better done, with moldings above and below. Above the bench a cornice $\frac{1}{2}$ foot deep and $2\frac{1}{4}$ feet wide made of solid wall was to surround the chapel as well as the entrance pilasters. The backrest, 3 feet high, was to contain 20 small coffered pilasters $2\frac{1}{2}$ feet in height. Between each of the pilasters there was to be represented a small door from which was to issue a *putto* 3 feet tall holding a torch, of which there should be 17 in all. On each of the three sides of each of the pilasters the backrest was to contain a Roman garland instead of *putti*. Above the backrest there was to be a cornice $\frac{1}{2}$ foot deep and $2\frac{1}{4}$ feet wide above which there were to rest 12 columns $5\frac{1}{2}$ feet high with capitals and bases. Half of them were to be twisted and half, fluted. On them were to be seated nude *putti* which, standing, should measure 2 feet in height. Between the columns and pilasters there were to be 16 niches of such a size that a figure 5 feet tall, carved in the round, might stand within them. In these niches there were to stand statues of the 12 Apostles plus 4 other figures. Between the Apostles there was to be constructed a square framed opening ("casamento"), 7 feet on each side, for a figure of Christ $5\frac{1}{4}$ feet high holding back two angels each 2 feet high and two further angels 3 feet high. In the same course of wall there were to be 2 candelabra on either side. Above the niches and *putti* there was to be a cornice $\frac{3}{4}$ foot deep, of which one third was not to project. Above this there was to run a course $2\frac{3}{4}$ feet high with 20 fluted pilasters of the same height flanking 17 oculi. The oculi, whose openings should measure $1\frac{1}{4}$ feet in diameter, were to be surrounded by rings containing a Roman festoon with suitable fruits and leaves. In this course there were to be 3 vases for each of the 2 pilasters on the entrance wall. Above the oculi there was to run a large cornice $1\frac{1}{4}$ feet in depth, made of two pieces, whose upper half was to be 3 feet wide. It was to surround the entire chapel including the pilasters at the entrance. Above this cornice on the north wall there was to be an arch, embellished with moldings and a festoon, whose opening should measure 13 feet. Within the field contained by this arch there was to be carved the Coronation of the Virgin in more than half relief. Standing, the figures of God the Father and the Madonna should measure $5\frac{1}{2}$ feet. They were to be surrounded by a choir of angels. Opposite this, above the entrance, there was to be an arch similar to the one surrounding the Coronation. The barrel vault was to rest on these arches and on the large cornice. It was to be coffered with squares of about 2 feet each and each coffer was to contain a seraph. In the center of the vault there was to be a half-length figure of God the Father within a ring which should occupy the space of 4 coffers.

The 3 exterior facades of the chapel were to be treated like the walls of the Cathedral. The stone that would be removed between the pilasters at the entrance to the chapel might be employed providing that it be recarved to match the new stone. The chapel was to be roofed with tiles on top of wood set above a cornice.

All the stone for the interior of the chapel was to come from the site in Voluje that would be designated by the administrator. The stone for the exterior might come from the island of Bua or any other place that Aleši and Niccolò might choose.

The proportions, gestures, movements and faces of the figures were to suit their age so that decorum should not be wanting. If one of the two partners should be missing, the other one was obligated to find a substitute who would engage himself jointly to complete the work. Meanwhile ser Nicolò promised, in the name of the administration, to demolish the house that stood on the building site at the due time and at the Cathedral's expense. He promised to give the sculptors the shrine of the saint in the church and the stone from the wall to be demolished between the entrance pilasters. He also promised that they might quarry stone in Voluje without payment of any tax and that they might have free use of the road to the dock. He further promised to provide two workshops in the cemetery in front of the portico: the old one he promised to fix up and the new one for the carving of the statues he promised to construct so that it would be entirely closed. The masters might use the house in which Aleši was then living until they wanted to lay the foundations. For their work the masters were to receive 2,300 ducats according to the following schedule. At the end of the coming March they were to receive all the money accruing from the bequest of the late Antonio Maçchusich and 50 ducats every four months thereafter, provided that they had executed an equivalent amount of work. If the masters should finish the work before they were obligated to do so, they would thereupon be paid in entirety. (*Ibid.*, pp. 74ff., doc. VII.) April 26, 1468 Niccolò gave a receipt for a payment of 70 ducats for works in connection with the chapel to be constructed. (*Ibid.*, pp. 77, doc. IX.) March 6, 1470 Niccolò, dwelling in Trogir, accepted an apprentice. (*Ibid.*, p. 77, doc. XIV.) May 30, 1470 Petar Juanni Grubissich of Brać made a receipt for 24 lire *di piccoli* received from Niccolò, living in Trogir, in partial payment for work of stonemasonry executed for Niccolò. At the same time Petar promised to work for Niccolò at the quarry in exchange for 18 lire *di piccoli* for a single month's work. Further, Petar was obliged to come to work within the next eight days. (*Ibid.*, p. 78, doc. XVI.) February 17, 1472 At Trogir, Aleši named Stefan Testa, citizen of Trogir, procurator for himself and Niccolò Fiorentino, instructing him to draw up the accounts in connection with the work for the Chapel of Beato Giovanni Orsini and to present it to the administration of the Cathedral. (Kukuljević, *Slovnik umjetnikah jugoslavenskih*, i, p. 8.) December 1, 1472 Niccolò's presence was recorded in Trogir. (Kolendić, *Arkhiv*, 1924, p. 78, doc. XVIII.) November 24, 1475 Aleši and Niccolò, partners, lodged a second complaint with the count of Trogir against ser Giovanni de Andreis, administrator of the Cathedral. They claimed that they had not been paid according to the terms of their contract by ser Giovanni's predecessor which was causing a loss of time and preventing them from finishing the work. They stated that ser Giovanni should give them two ducats every day starting that very day until he had given them an amount of money equivalent to the amount of work that they had finished up to that day. They also requested that ser Giovanni consign to them the place where the foundations of the chapel were to be laid, that the old workshop be fixed and that the shed of boards be made in such a way that the works would not get wet. (Fisković, JAZU. Inst. za likovne umjetnosti. *Bulletin*, 1959, p. 42, n. 16.) This document contradicts the evidence contained in the report of the visitation of the Cathedral made by Didaco Manola, bishop of Trogir, on May 31, 1756, which in other respects seems to be accurate and was evidently based on a perusal of documents which have not yet come to light. In his report, Manola stated that the foundation of the new chapel was laid in 1468. He also stated that in the same year the earlier Chapel of Blessed Giovanni Orsini on the site of the new chapel was demolished. (Fisković, *Opis trogirske katedrale*, p. 41.) 1477 As a member of the board of works, Coriolano Cippico gave Nicolò Lipavich a house over which the Cathedral exercised property rights in exchange for certain places which Lipavich owned surrounding the site of the new Chapel of Blessed Giovanni Orsini. (*Ibid.*, p. 41.) July 1,

1477 In the contract in which Niccolò was named *protomaestro* of the Cathedral of Šibenik, permission was granted him to go to Trogir for two or three days at a time whenever his business interests should require. (Frey-Molè, p. 161, doc. 144.) 1482 The statue of *St. John the Evangelist* was delivered for a price of 186 lire, 4 soldi. (Fisković, *Opis trogirske katedrale*, p. 43. This information is confirmed by Giovanni Lucio, *Memorie istoriche di Tragurio*, Venice, 1673, p. 487.) 1487 Statues of *Our Lord*, the *Virgin Mary*, and *St. Peter* were carved by Niccolò Fiorentino for a total price of 673 lire, 16 soldi equal to 224 lire, 12 soldi for each statue. (*Ibid.*, p. 43.) 1488 Niccolò Fiorentino finished the statue of *St. John the Baptist* for a price of 155 lire. (*Ibid.*, pp. 43f.) 1489 Another four statues were carved by Niccolò at a price of 155 lire per statue. (*Ibid.*, p. 44.) 1494 The statue of *Jesus Christ* was finished for a price of 155 lire. (*Ibid.*, p. 44.) February 12, 1497 From the contract in which Niccolò's tenure as *protomaestro* of the Cathedral of Šibenik was renewed we learn that Niccolò was still under obligation to the Cathedral of Trogir and that the figures for the chapel were not yet finished. In the contract, Niccolò was specifically granted permission to bring and work on a stone figure, either alone or together with his son in order to teach him how to carve the figure. In the city, they might do that work either at the quarry or in the stone workshop, provided that the workmen at the Cathedral had been told what to do in Niccolò's absence so that they would not waste time. (Kolendić, *Glasnik*, 1925, p. 207, n. 4.) 1508 One statue was finished by "Magistro Joanne lapicida" for 155 lire. (Fisković, *Opis trogirske katedrale*, p. 44.) A second statue of *St. John the Evangelist* is inscribed "IOANNIS · DAMATAE · F ·." (Cvito Fisković, "Djela kipara Ivana Duknovića u Trogiru," *Historijski zbornik* [Zagreb], iii, 1950, p. 234.) The statue of *St. Thomas* also shows the influence of Giovanni Dalmata. February 22, 1524 Contract with Antonio Fiorentino for the construction of the altar of the chapel for 35 ducats. Antonio's death prevented the fulfilment of the contract. (Fisković, *Opis trogirske katedrale*, p. 42.) 1559 Four statues still missing from the chapel were furnished for 313 lire, 2 soldi each. (*Ibid.*, p. 44.) These are probably the four statues attributed to Alessandro Vittoria by Vasari and located today at the four angles of the base of the pyramid of the Campanile at Trogir. (Kruno Prijatelj, "Alessandro Vittoria e la Dalmazia," *Arte veneta*, xii, 1958, pp. 205ff.) May 4, 1681 The body of Orsini was translated from the Altar of the Crucifix to the chapel. (Paolo Andreis, "Traslazione di San Giovanni Vescovo di Traù fatta li 4 maggio l'anno 1681," *Archivio storico per la Dalmazia*, iii, 1927, fasc. 18, pp. 281–292; iv, 1927, fasc. 19, pp. 41–52; iv, 1927, fasc. 21, pp. 149–156; iv, 1928, fasc. 23, pp. 248–254; iv, 1928, fasc. 24, pp. 299–306.) (For the history of the chapel in the seventeenth and eighteenth centuries see: Lucio, *Memorie istoriche di Tragurio*, 1673, pp. 488ff.; Fisković, *Opis trogirske katedrale* [1756], pp. 41ff.; Daniele Farlati, *Illyricum sacrum*, Venice, iv, 1769, pp. 429, 435ff., 444; Fisković, "Ignacije Macanović i njegov krug," *Prilozi povijesti umjetnosti u Dalmaciji* [Split], ix, 1955, p. 258, n. 117.)

CAMPANILE OF S. DOIMO, SPLIT

November 30, 1472 In his own name and that of Niccolò, Aleši made a final quittance for 90 ducats which he and Niccolò had received according to their contract in payment for changing certain columns and other work on the Campanile of the Duomo, Split. (Praga, *Rassegna marchigiana*, 1929–30, p. 16, doc. 27.)

FACADE OF S. MARIA, ISLAND OF S. NICCOLÒ, TREMITI ARCHIPELAGO

October 20, 1473 Don Ambrogio da Milano, prior of the Augustinian monastery attached to the church of S. Maria on the island of S. Niccolò in the Tremiti archipelago, promised to send Andrea Aleši, by the next feast day of the Presentation of the Virgin (November 21), 38 ducats as his portion of what remained to be paid of the 700 ducats promised him and his partner, Niccolò Fiorentino, for the construction of the facade of the church. If it should be discovered that more money had been disbursed to the masters or their families or the masters who were working with them for the preceding three months than the 12 ducats, 4 lire, 14 soldi recorded in the accounts, half of that amount would be subtracted from the 38 ducats due Aleši. (Kolendic, *Glasnik*, 1925, p. 210, doc. II.) October 20, 1473 Niccolò was also promised the same sum with the same conditions, but he was not to receive his money until Easter (April 10, 1474). (*Ibid.*, p. 210, doc. II.) July 27, 1474 Decision in Rome of Pope Sixtus IV in response to the complaint of Aleši and Niccolò that they had not received the 76 ducats due them for the completed work of the facade of S. Maria. The pope ordered that the matter be resolved by Bishop Biagio from Otok who was substituting for the archbishop of Split. (*Ibid.*, p. 209, doc. II.) February 27, 1475 Aleši gave a receipt at Split in his name and that of his partner, Niccolò, for 46 ducats received from the steward of the monastery for their work. (*Ibid.*, p. 208, doc. I; p. 210, doc. II.) May 5, 1479 The procurator of the monastery was summoned to the first session of court to be held at Split following the feast day of St. Domnius. (*Ibid.*, pp. 208f., doc. II.) May 15, 1479 In spite of the absence of the procurator of the monastery or any substitute, the documents described above were presented as evidence. Through their procurators, Aleši and Niccolò demanded, in addition to the remaining 30 ducats due them, a further 66 ducats, 4 lire, 3 soldi for expenses of travel and transport as well as legal expenses. Eight ducats were requested for two *putti* placed at the summit of the portal which had not been included in the original design. (*Ibid.*, pp. 209ff., doc. II.) May 17, 1479 Bishop Biagio sentenced the procurator of the monastery, still absent, to pay Aleši and Niccolò the 30 ducats still due them as part of the original agreement plus 35 ducats, 4 lire for their expenses and interest. (*Ibid.*, p. 211, doc. II.) June 17, 1479 Summoned before the judge, the lawyer for the monastery stated his intention of appealing Bishop Biagio's sentence to the apostolic seat. Aleši and Niccolò presented a reduced list of expenses to the amount of 49 ducats, 1 lira, 12 soldi. The judge ordered that the list be given the lawyer and that he have until the following Monday to make any objection to it. (*Ibid.*, pp. 211ff., doc. II.) June 21, 1479 The procurator of the monastery replied that the second list of demands was nul because, having once heard the case and issued a sentence which was in the process of being appealed, the bishop no longer had jurisdiction in the case. (*Ibid.*, p. 213, doc. II.) June 23, 1479 Objecting that the trial had not yet taken place, Aleši and Niccolò's procurator asked the judge to proceed to the administration of justice. (*Ibid.*, pp. 213f., doc. II.) August 9, 1479 A sentence, apparently in Aleši's and Niccolò's favor, was issued by Bishop Biagio. (Praga, *Rassegna marchigiana*, 1929–30, p. 22, doc. 53.) February 23, 1480 Aleši and Niccolò agreed on three arbiters who would judge the dispute concerning the expenses and the controversies which had arisen between them as a result of their lawsuit with the monastery of S. Maria. Whatever amount Niccolò should be judged as owing, Andrea might take from the sum of money which the monastery still owed Niccolò and which was in the possession of ser Battista da Eugubio. (Kolendić, *Glasnik*, 1925, p. 214, doc. III.) March 22, 1480 The two procurators of the monastery of S. Maria claimed the sentence issued by Bishop Biagio on August 9, 1479, to have been obtained by fraudulent misrepresentation, but in order to avoid further labor and expense, they therewith made an agreement with Aleši. Andrea declared himself content to receive 12 ducats out of the money sequestered and in the possession of ser Battista da Eugubio. These 12 ducats were the final payment owed to Andrea for his salary, legal expenses connected with the lawsuit, and other things. For their part, the procurators promised Andrea to defend him from any claim for expenses made against him by Niccolò Fiorentino. Andrea further promised not to trouble Niccolò concerning the expenses of the lawsuit or anything else. (Praga, *Rassegna marchigiana*, 1929–30, pp. 21f., doc. 53.) March 23, 1480 With the agreement of Aleši and Niccolò's procurator, ser Battista da Eugubio gave the two procurators of the monastery of S. Maria 318 lire, 2 soldi for which a receipt was drawn up. (*Ibid.*, pp. 22f., doc. 54.)

CATHEDRAL OF ŠIBENIK

By October 16, 1475 Niccolò had succeeded Giorgio da Sebenico, who had died on October 10, 1473, as *protomaestro* of the Cathedral of S. Giacomo at Šibenik. (Kolendić, *Starinar*, 1923, p. 91, n. 164.) October 23 and 24, 1476; February 11, 1477 Niccolò received his salary as architect of the Cathedral. (*Ibid.*, p. 94.) July 1, 1477 Niccolò was appointed *protomaestro* for the following ten years to be measured from May 1, 1477, with the following conditions: during that period the administration might not appoint another *protomaestro*, nor might Niccolò obligate himself as *protomaestro* to any other person: within four months of having been summoned, Niccolò should have to come to work; Niccolò was given up to three months' leave during the summer in order to go to attend to his other work; Niccolò was given leave to go to Trogir or elsewhere for two or three days at a time when his business required; on holidays Niccolò was not obligated to work; Niccolò's salary of ten ducats per month was to be paid every two months when Niccolò was working for the church; from time to time, or whenever Niccolò had been given leave, his accounts were to be rendered and all money due him, paid. Both parties agreed to abide by the conditions under a penalty of a quarter of the money and to make good all expenses of litigation. (Frey-Molè, pp. 160f., doc. 144.) January 7, 1479 Niccolò gave a receipt for his salary received during the tenure as procurator of the Cathedral of ser Paolo Petrovich. (*Ibid.*, p. 161, doc. 147.) November 24, 1483 Niccolò received an apprentice for two years. (*Ibid.*, p. 162, doc. 149.) Between 1486 and 1489 Niccolò added the tabernacles to the main portal of the Cathedral. (Kolendić, *Narodna starina*, 1924, p. 175.) April 2, 1493 Niccolò was made procurator of the Cathedral in order to prosecute those people responsible for the illegal seizure of the Cathedral's quarry at Brać. (Frey-Molè, p. 163, doc. 157.) February 12, 1497 Niccolò's contract as *protomaestro* of the Cathedral was renewed for the following ten years. (Kolendić, *Glasnik*, 1925, p. 207, n. 4.) January 25, 1499 Niccolò was commissioned to execute the balustrades composed of twisted colonettes in the three apses of the east end of the Cathedral. With the exception of copper and lead, all expenses were to be borne by him. Niccolò was to receive

100 ducats to be paid during the progress of the work. For 20 ducats of his stipend, received on this occasion, Niccolò gave a receipt to the procurator, ser Mario. Both parties agreed to abide by the conditions of the contract under a penalty of a quarter of the price and to make good all expenses of litigation. (Frey-Molè, p. 164, doc. 159.)

BALUSTRADE FOR THE STAIRS OF S. GIOVANNI BATTISTA, ŠIBENIK

October 16, 1475 Niccolò was commissioned by Giacomello Michaelis, representative of the Confraternity of S. Giovanni di Monte in the church of S. Trinita (later S. Giovanni Battista), to construct the balustrade for the stairs of the fraternity in accordance with a drawing given to Giacomello. (The exterior staircase leading from the street to the *cantoria* of the church had been erected between 1460 and 1461 by Giovanni Pribislavlich: Kolendić, *Starinar*, 1923, pp. 65f.) Niccolò was obligated to make the balustrade of good stone entirely at his own expense in exchange for 26 ducats. One hundred and ten lire *di piccoli* were given to him on this occasion. The rest would be given to him when the work was completed. (*Ibid.*, p. 91, n. 164.)

CHAPEL OF S. MARIA, METAJNA, PAG

On the facade of the chapel of S. Maria at Metajna on the island of Pag is the following inscription: "MCCCCLXXXVII. ME. FECIT MR. / NICOLAUS SIBENICI. . . ." (Felicinović, *Narodna Politika*, June 12, 1928, p. 2.) The identification of this Master Niccolò from Šibenik with Niccolò di Giovanni (Krsto Stošić, *Galerija uglednih Šibenčana*, Šibenik, 1936, p. 28.) has yet to be confirmed.

WINDOWS FOR THE COURTYARD OF THE MONASTERY OF S. CRISOGONO, ZADAR

October 24, 1485 Deodato Venier, abbot of the monastery of S. Crisogono, Zadar, commissioned Niccolò, at that time sojourning in Zadar, to make certain stone windows with their proportionate embellishments and figures for the courtyard of the monastery in front of the abbot's room. The design of the windows was to accord with a drawing on sheets of papyrus which might remain in Niccolò's possession. The work was to be finished, transported to Zadar and delivered to the monastery by August 31, 1486 and installed by October 31, 1486. Niccolò was to bear the expense of all work and material with the exception of lime and sand, all contrivances necessary for hoisting the stones and the preparation of the internal side of the wall. For his work Niccolò was to receive 134 ducats of which he received 34 ducats on this occasion as a deposit for the work. (Prijatelj, *Prilozi povijesti umjetnosti u Dalmaciji*, 1961, pp. 227f., n. 1.)

S. MARIA DI VALVERDE, ŠIBENIK

January 10, 1502 Niccolò, called citizen of Šibenik, was appointed *protomaestro* of the church of S. Maria di Valverde, Šibenik, for the following five years by the procurators of the Confraternity of S. Maria di Valverde and the administrators of the church. During that time he was to oversee personally the quarrying of stone and the construction of the church, for which he would be paid 10 ducats per month. He was given leave to absent himself from work for three days each month in order to attend to his own business. All those masters who would assist him in quarrying stone, laying foundations, and constructing the building were to be paid according to their contracts. Before the expiration of Niccolò's term, no other *protomaestro* might be appointed. (Frey-Molè, p. 165, doc. 162.) January 20, 1502 Niccolò took up his appointment as *protomaestro*. (Miagostovich, *I nobili e il clero di Sebenico*, p. 63.) April 12, 1502 Niccolò traveled to Brać for the quarrying of stone for the church. (*Ibid.*, p. 63.) June 15, 1503 Niccolò was sent 60 lire by one of the procurators of S. Maria di Valverde. (*Ibid.*, p. 63.) May 31, 1505 Niccolò received two months' salary. (*Ibid.*, p. 63.) January 1, 1506 The administrators of the church made an agreement with Master Mihajlo Hreljić for a great quantity of material. It is therefore likely that by this time Niccolò was dead. (Kolendić, *Starinar*, 1923, p. 91, n. 168.) Niccolò was survived by three sons, Masters Jacopo, Anticcio, and Zuanne. Jacopo and Anticcio were sculptors. Zuanne, a hunchback, was a goldsmith. In 1502 all three were employed at S. Maria di Valverde. August 13, 1502 Zuanne Gobbo received from the church 24 lire's worth of cloth for which he promised to execute an equivalent amount of goldsmithery. (Miagostovich, *I nobili e il clero di Sebenico*, p. 63; Kolendić, *Glasnik*, 1925, p. 207.)

Illustrations

2. Arco Foscari, Ducal Palace, Venice

1. Niccolò di Giovanni and assistant, Foscari Tomb, S. Maria dei Frari, Venice

3. Niccolò di Giovanni, detail, *Charity* from the Foscari Tomb, S. Maria dei Frari, Venice

4. Niccolò di Giovanni, detail, *Faith* from the Foscari Tomb, S. Maria dei Frari, Venice

5. Niccolò di Giovanni, *Charity* from the Foscari Tomb, S. Maria dei Frari, Venice

6. Niccolò di Giovanni, *Faith* from the Foscari Tomb, S. Maria dei Frari, Venice

7. Niccolò di Giovanni, detail, *Hope* from the Foscari Tomb, S. Maria dei Frari, Venice

8. Niccolò di Giovanni, *St. Francis* or *St. Anthony of Padua* from the Foscari Tomb, S. Maria dei Frari, Venice

9. Niccolò di Giovanni, *Hope* from the Foscari Tomb, S. Maria dei Frari, Venice

10. Niccolò di Giovanni, *St. Mark* from the Foscari Tomb, S. Maria dei Frari, Venice

12. Assistant of Niccolò di Giovanni, right-hand *Warrior* from the Foscari Tomb, S. Maria dei Frari, Venice

11. Niccolò di Giovanni, left-hand *Warrior* from the Foscari Tomb, S. Maria dei Frari, Venice

14. Assistant of Niccolò di Giovanni, detail, right-hand *Warrior* from the Foscari Tomb, S. Maria dei Frari, Venice

13. Niccolò di Giovanni, detail, left-hand *Warrior* from the Foscari Tomb, S. Maria dei Frari, Venice

16. Niccolò di Giovanni, *Justice* and *Prudence* from the Foscari Tomb, S. Maria dei Frari, Venice

15. Niccolò di Giovanni and assistant, *Fortitude* and *Temperance* from the Foscari Tomb, S. Maria dei Frari, Venice

18. Niccolò di Giovanni, *Justice* and *Prudence* from the Foscari Tomb, S. Maria dei Frari, Venice

17. Niccolò di Giovanni and assistant, *Fortitude* from the Foscari Tomb, S. Maria dei Frari, Venice

19. Niccolò di Giovanni, detail, *Justice* from the Foscari Tomb, S. Maria dei Frari, Venice

20. Niccolò di Giovanni, detail, *Prudence* from the Foscari Tomb, S. Maria dei Frari, Venice

21. Assistant of Niccolò di Giovanni, detail, *Temperance* from the Foscari Tomb, S. Maria dei Frari, Venice

22. Assistant of Niccolò di Giovanni, detail, *Fortitude* from the Foscari Tomb, S. Maria dei Frari, Venice

23. Niccolò di Giovanni, detail, *Christ Ascending into Glory* from the Foscari Tomb, S. Maria dei Frari, Venice

24. Niccolò di Giovanni, detail, *Effigy* from the Foscari Tomb, S. Maria dei Frari, Venice

25. Niccolò di Giovanni, detail, *Angel Gabriel* from the Foscari Tomb, S. Maria dei Frari, Venice

26. Niccolò di Giovanni, detail, *Virgin Annunciate* from the Foscari Tomb, S. Maria dei Frari, Venice

28. Niccolò di Giovanni, *Christ Ascending into Glory* from the Foscari Tomb, S. Maria dei Frari, Venice

27. Niccolò di Giovanni, *Christ Ascending into Glory* from the Foscari Tomb, S. Maria dei Frari, Venice

30. Niccolò di Giovanni, *Virgin Annunciate* from the Foscari Tomb, S. Maria dei Frari, Venice

29. Niccolò di Giovanni, *Angel Gabriel* from the Foscari Tomb, S. Maria dei Frari, Venice

31. Niccolò di Giovanni, *Effigy* from the Foscari Tomb, S. Maria dei Frari, Venice

32. Niccolò di Giovanni, detail, *Christ Ascending into Glory* from the
Foscari Tomb, S. Maria dei Frari, Venice

33. Niccolò di Giovanni, detail, *Christ
Ascending into Glory* from the
Foscari Tomb, S. Maria dei Frari,
Venice

34. Johannes Grevembroch, *Doge Moro Kneeling before the Lion of St. Mark*
from the Arco Foscari (*Monumenta Veneta ex antiquis ruderibus*, ii, p. 50)

35. Assistant of Niccolò di Giovanni, *St.
Mark* from the Arco Foscari, Ducal
Palace, Venice

36. Assistant of Niccolò di Giovanni,
Gorgon Warrior from the Arco
Foscari, Ducal Palace, Venice

37. Female statues from the Arco Foscari, Ducal Palace, Venice

39. Niccolò di Giovanni, *Moro Warrior* from the Arco Foscari, Ducal Palace, Venice

38. Niccolò di Giovanni, *Moro Warrior* from the Arco Foscari, Ducal Palace, Venice

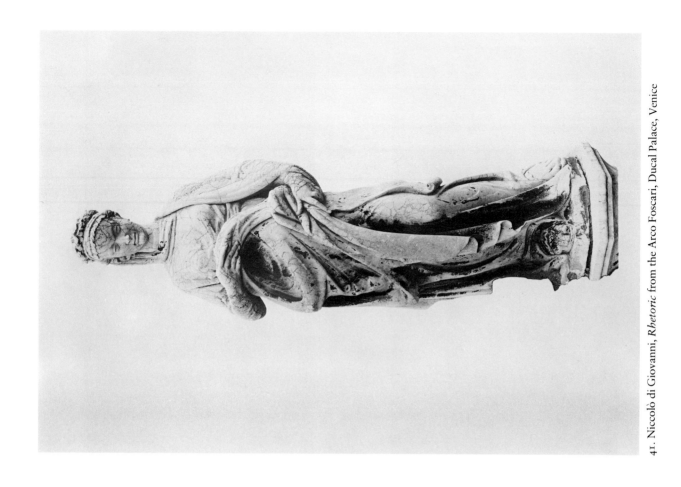

41. Niccolò di Giovanni, *Rhetoric* from the Arco Foscari, Ducal Palace, Venice

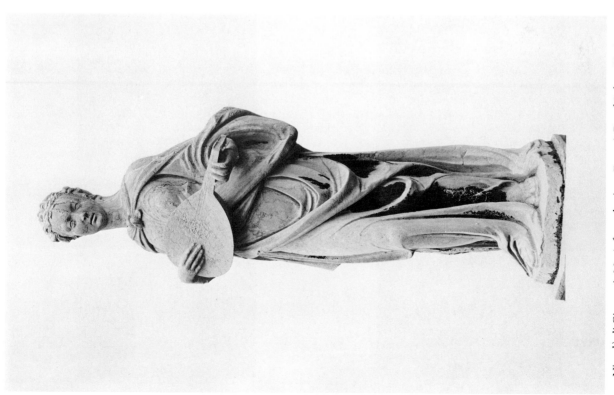

40. Niccolò di Giovanni, *Music* from the Arco Foscari, Ducal Palace, Venice

42. Assistant of Niccolò di Giovanni, *Charity* from the Giustiniani Tomb, Kress Collection, Museum of Art, El Paso, Texas

43. Assistant of Niccolò di Giovanni, *Temperance* from the Giustiniani Tomb, Kress Collection, Museum of Art, El Paso, Texas

44. Assistant of Niccolò di Giovanni, *Fortitude* from the Giustiniani Tomb, Cassa di Risparmio di Padova e Rovigo, Padua

45. Assistant of Niccolò di Giovanni, *Virtue* from the Giustiniani Tomb, Cassa di Risparmio di Padova e Rovigo, Padua

47. Johannes Grevembroch, *Giustiniani Tomb*, S. Andrea della Certosa, Venice (*Monumenta Veneta ex antiquis ruderibus*, i, p. 92)

46. Assistant of Niccolò di Giovanni, *Hope* from the Giustiniani Tomb, Metropolitan Museum of Art, New York

48. Niccolò di Giovanni, Capello Tomb, S. Elena, Venice

49. Niccolò di Giovanni, detail, *St. Helen* from the Capello Tomb, S. Elena, Venice

50. Assistant of Niccolò di Giovanni, detail,
Temperance from the Giustiniani Tomb, Kress
Collection, Museum of Art, El Paso, Texas

51. Niccolò di Giovanni, detail, *St. Helen* from the Capello
Tomb, S. Elena, Venice

52. Assistant of Niccolò di Giovanni, detail,
Temperance from the Giustiniani Tomb, Kress
Collection, Museum of Art, El Paso, Texas

53. Niccolò di Giovanni, detail, *St. Helen* from the Capello
Tomb, S. Elena, Venice

54. Assistant of Niccolò di Giovanni, detail, *Temperance* from the Giustiniani Tomb, Kress Collection, Museum of Art, El Paso, Texas

55. Niccolò di Giovanni, detail, *St. Helen* from the Capello Tomb, S. Elena, Venice

56. Niccolò di Giovanni, detail, *Vittore Capello* from the Capello Tomb, S. Elena, Venice

57. Niccolò di Giovanni, detail, *Vittore Capello* from the Capello Tomb, S. Elena, Venice

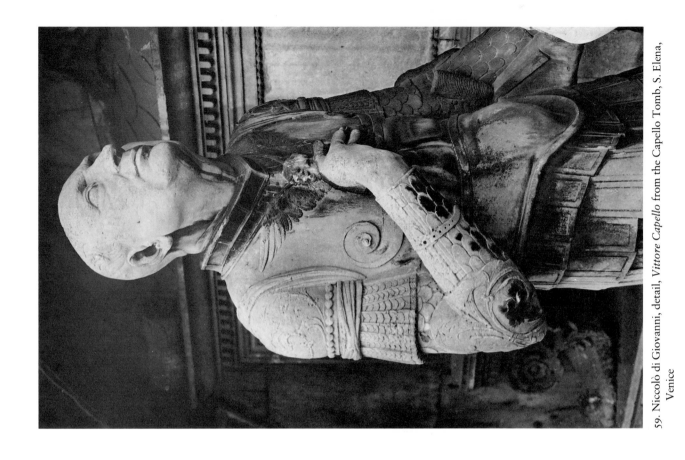

59. Niccolò di Giovanni, detail, *Vittore Capello* from the Capello Tomb, S. Elena, Venice

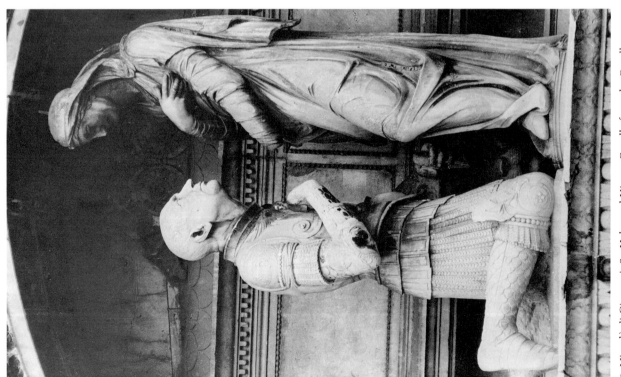

58. Niccolò di Giovanni, *St. Helen* and *Vittore Capello* from the Capello Tomb, S. Elena, Venice

61. Niccolò di Giovanni, detail, *Vittore Capello* from the Capello Tomb, S. Elena, Venice

60. Niccolò di Giovanni, detail, *Vittore Capello* from the Capello Tomb, S. Elena, Venice

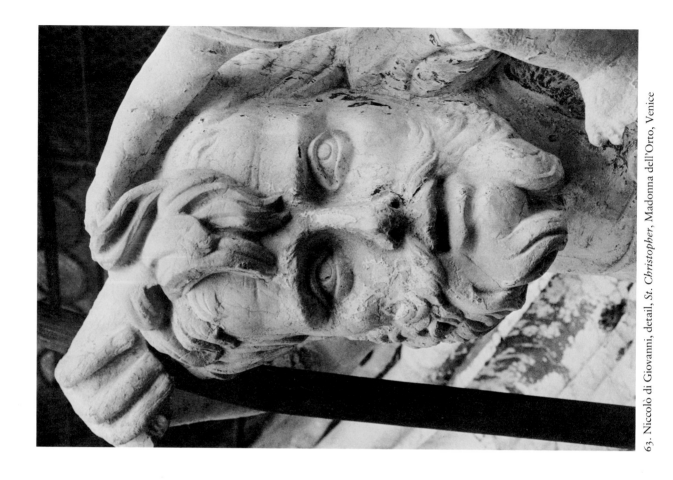

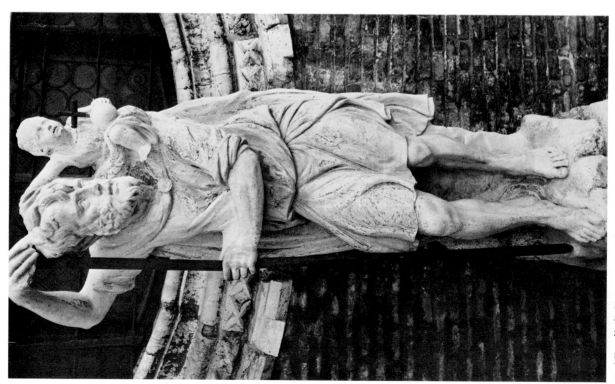

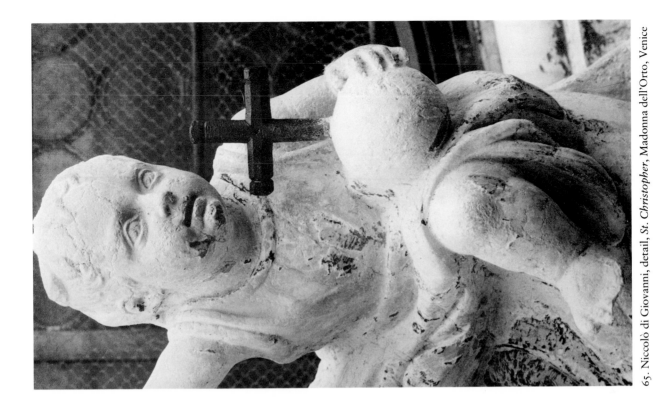

65. Niccolò di Giovanni, detail, *St. Christopher*, Madonna dell'Orto, Venice

64. Niccolò di Giovanni, detail, *St. Christopher*, Madonna dell'Orto, Venice

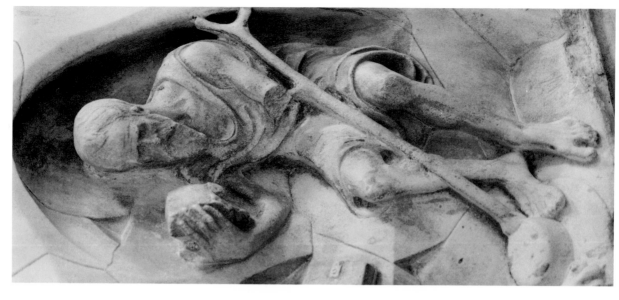

67. Niccolò di Giovanni, detail, *St. Jerome in the Desert*, S. Maria del Giglio, Venice

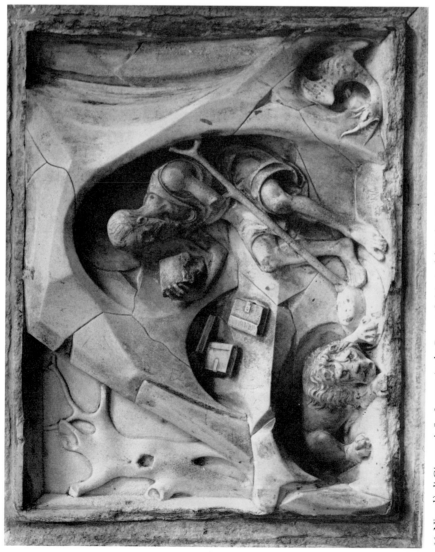

66. Niccolò di Giovanni, *St. Jerome in the Desert*, S. Maria del Giglio, Venice

68. Andrea Mantegna, *Resurrection of Christ*, Musée des Beaux-Arts, Tours

69. Bartolomeo Vivarini, *Ascension of Christ* from the Altarpiece of St. Andrew, Rab, Museum of Fine Arts, Boston

72. Antonio Rizzo, detail, *Eve*, Ducal Palace, Venice

71. Venetian gold ducat from the reign of Doge Foscari

70. Antonio Rizzo, *St. Paul* from the Altar of St. Paul, S. Marco, Venice

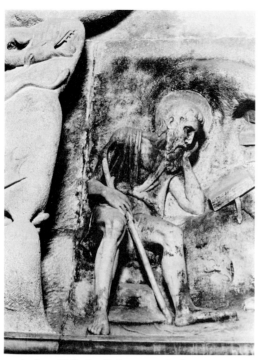

73. Andrea Aleši, detail, *St. Jerome in the Desert*, Baptistry, Trogir

74. Andrea Aleši, *St. Jerome in the Desert*, St. Jerome, Marjan (Split)

75. Andrea Aleši, *St. Jerome in the Desert*, Walker Art Gallery, Liverpool

76. Niccolò di Giovanni, *St. Jerome in the Desert*, Society of Friends of Ragusan Antiquities, Dubrovnik

77. Niccolò di Giovanni, detail,
Lamentation, St. John the Baptist,
Trogir

78. Niccolò di Giovanni, *Lamentation*, St. John the Baptist, Trogir

79. Niccolò di Giovanni, detail, *Lamentation*, St. John the
Baptist, Trogir

80. Niccolò di Giovanni, detail, *Lamentation*, St. John the
Baptist, Trogir

81. Niccolò di Giovanni, left-hand *Genius*, Palace of
Coriolano Cippico, Trogir

82. Niccolò di Giovanni, right-hand *Genius*, Palace of
Coriolano Cippico, Trogir

83. Niccolò di Giovanni, *Torch-bearing putto* from the
Orsini Chapel, Cathedral, Trogir

84. Niccolò di Giovanni, *God the Father*, Cathedral,
Šibenik

85. Assistant of Niccolò di Giovanni, left-hand *Angel*, Cathedral, Šibenik

86. Assistant of Niccolò di Giovanni, right-hand *Angel*, Cathedral, Šibenik

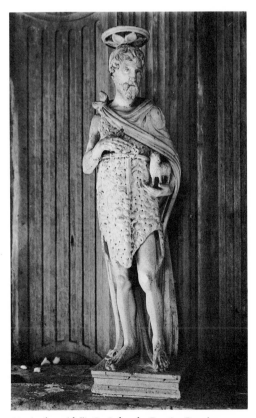

87. Niccolò di Giovanni, *St. John the Baptist*, St. John the Baptist, Šibenik

88. Andrea Aleši, *St. John the Baptist*, Baptistry, Trogir

89. Assistant of Niccolò di Giovanni, *St. James*,
Cathedral, Šibenik

90. Niccolò di Giovanni and assistant, Sobota Tomb, St. Dominic, Trogir

91. Assistant of Niccolò di Giovanni, *St. James* from
the Orsini Chapel, Cathedral, Trogir

92. Assistant of Niccolò di Giovanni, detail, *Lamentation* from the
Sobota Tomb, St. Dominic, Trogir

93. Niccolò di Giovanni, detail, *Resurrected Christ* from the Orsini Chapel, Cathedral, Trogir

94. Niccolò di Giovanni, *Resurrected Christ* from the Orsini Chapel, Cathedral, Trogir

95. Niccolò di Giovanni, *Putto* from the Orsini Chapel, Cathedral, Trogir

96. Assistant of Niccolò di Giovanni, *Christ Ascending into Glory*, Cemetery, Trogir

97. Niccolò di Giovanni, *St. Michael*, Cathedral, Šibenik

98. Niccolò di Giovanni, detail, *St. Sebastian*, Muzej grada, Trogir

99. Niccolò di Giovanni, detail, *Coronation of the Virgin* from the Orsini Chapel, Cathedral, **Trogir**

100. Niccolò di Giovanni, *Coronation of the Virgin* from the Orsini Chapel, Cathedral, Trogir

Index

ni), 21f., 25, 27, 28, 35, 36, 41 n. 44, 52, 60, Fig. 41; *St. Mark* (shop of Niccolò di Giovanni), 20, 22, 36, 41 n. 44, 52, 56, 61, Fig. 35; *Worshiping Youths*, 44 n. 72, 63 n. 3; east wing (Antonio Rizzo), 30, 53; *Eve* (Antonio Rizzo), 47 n. 96, 53, 54, Fig. 72; loggia, *Bust of a Doge*, 41 n. 50; "Mars," (Antonio Rizzo), 41 n. 42, 54; Museo dell'Opera, *Portrait of Doge Francesco Foscari* from the Porta della Carta, Ducal Palace, Venice (Bartolomeo Bon), 63 n. 3; Porta della Carta (Giovanni and Bartolomeo Bon and shop), 9, 19; *Virtues*, 41 n. 44; *Charity*, 24, 43 n. 64, 63 n. 3; *Fortitude* (Bartolomeo Bon), 39 n. 29, 51, 63 n. 3; *Prudence*, 63 n. 3; *Temperance* (Bartolomeo Bon), 39 n. 29, 51, 63 n. 3; Porticato della Carta, 9, 18f.; Sala del Piovego, 9; Scala dei Giganti (Antonio Rizzo), 53; west wing, 9
——, Frezzaria, 67 n. 44
——, Libreria, 67 n. 44
——, Madonna dell'Orto, portal (Bartolomeo Bon *et al.*), 4, 30f., 51; statues, 46 n. 94, 47 n. 101; *Gabriel*, 48 n. 106; *St. Christopher* (Niccolò di Giovanni), 5, 30–33, 34f., 36, 52, 58, 61f., 71, Figs. 62–65; *Virgin Annunciate*, 33, 41 n. 44
——, Merceria, 10
——, Museo Archeologico, *putti* from the "Throne of Saturn," 67f. n. 44
——, Museo Civico Correr, drawing of the Tomb of Doge Francesco Foscari at S. Maria dei Frari, Venice (Antonio Battisti), 39 n. 28
——, Palazzo Soranzo-van Axel, 5f.
——, Piazza S. Marco, 2, 67 n. 44
——, S. Alvise, *S. Alvise* (Bartolomeo Bon), 51
——, S. Andrea della Certosa (destroyed), Tomb of Ser Orsato Giustiniani (shop of Niccolò di Giovanni) (dispersed), 4, 5, 23–25, 27, 30, 35f., 41 n. 51, 52, 53, 71; drawing of, by Johannes Grevembroch, 23f., 53, Fig. 47; *Effigy* (lost), 44 n. 72, 53
——, S. Andrea della Zirada, 5
——, S. Aponal, 25
——, S. Cristoforo della Pace (destroyed), 2
——, S. Elena, Tomb of Vittore Capello (Niccolò di Giovanni), 4, 5, 25–30, 35, 36, 52, 53, 71, 72, Fig. 48; architecture, 30, 45 n. 79; *Capello*, 26f., 28–30, 54, 70, Figs. 56–61; drawing of, by Johannes Grevembroch, 26f., 45 n. 82, 46 ns. 89, 92; drawing of, by A. Mezzani, 46 n. 87; drawing of, by Querena, 46 n. 87; engraving of, by Dala, 46 n. 87; engraving of, by Musitelli, 46 n. 87;

iconography, 26f.; *St. Helen*, 26–28, 30, 32, 47 n. 101, 48 n. 106, Figs. 49, 51, 53, 55, 58; Tomb slab of Giacomo and Pietro Loredan, 8 n. 8
——, S. Francesco del Deserto, 2
——, S. Giobbe, 2; presbytery, 4
——, S. Giorgio in Alga (formerly), 2
——, SS. Giovanni e Paolo, 23, 25, 26, 36 n. 3; portal (Bartolomeo Bon *et al.*), 4, 5; Tomb of Doge Giovanni Mocenigo (Tullio Lombardo), 43 n. 64; Tomb of Doge Pietro Mocenigo (Pietro Lombardo), 4, 12; Tomb of Doge Tomaso Mocenigo (Pietro Lamberti and Giovanni di Martino da Fiesole), 12 f., 24, 71; Tomb of Agnese and Orsola Venier, 13; Tomb of Doge Antonio Venier, 13
——, S. Giovanni Elemosinario, Tomb of Paolo della Pergola (lost), 4
——, S. Giovanni in Bragora, 5
——, S. Giovanni in Olio, 2
——, S. Giuliano, Monument of Tommaso Rangone da Ravenna (Jacopo Sansovino), 26
——, S. Gregorio, 2, 7 n. 2; Tomb of Bartolomeo Morosini (Bartolomeo Bon and Guido Bianco Veneziano) (lost), 4
——, S. Marco, 19, 41 n. 51, 64 n. 10; Altars of SS. Paul, James and Clement (Antonio Rizzo), 4, 54, Fig. 70; Tomb of Cardinal Giambattista Zen (Paolo Savin), 24; west facade, *doccioni*, 13
——, S. Maria dei Frari, 10, 36 n. 3; Cappella Cornaro, Cenotaph of Federico Cornaro (Jacomo Padovano), 6, 8 n. 21, 41 n. 42, 44 n. 72; wall bench, 24; Cappella Maggiore, 10, 11; Cappella Miani, altarpiece, 7; Tomb of Bishop Pietro Miani, 4; choir screen, 4; *St. John the Baptist* (Donatello), 7; Tomb of Doge Francesco Foscari (Niccolò di Giovanni), 4, 5, 6, 9–18, 25, 27, 35, 44 n. 72, 47 ns. 96, 97, 52, 53, 57, 62, 71, Fig. 1; *Angel*, 11f., 13f., 32, 38f. n. 28, 61f., Figs. 32, 33; architecture, 18, 30, 37 n. 11; *Christ*, 11f., 13, 16, 20, 22, 29, 32, 61, 62, 70, Figs. 23, 27, 28; drawing of, by Antonio Battisti, 39 n. 28; drawing of, by Querena, 39 n. 28; *Effigy*, 11, 13, 14, 22, 29f., 32, 47 n. 96, 53, 70, Figs. 24, 31; engraving of, by Vincenzo Coronelli, 39 n. 28; engraving of, by Marco Sebastiano Giampiccoli, 14, 39 n. 29, 52, 53; engraving of, by Moretti, 39 n. 28; *Gabriel*, 11, 13, 15, 17f., 28, 40 n. 29, 46 n. 94, 47 n. 101, 48 n. 106, 58, Figs. 25, 29; iconography, 11–13; *putti* with Foscari arms, 11, 18; *St. Francis* or *St. Anthony of Padua*, 11, 61, Fig. 8; *St. Mark*, 11, 31f., Fig.